www.wadsworth.com

www.wadsworth.com is the World Wide Web site for Thomson Wadsworth and is your direct source to dozens of online resources.

At *www.wadsworth.com* you can find out about supplements, demonstration software, and student resources. You can also send email to many of our authors and preview new publications and exciting new technologies.

wadsworth.com
Changing the way the world learns®

CONTEMPORARY MORAL PROBLEMS

War and Terrorism

SECOND EDITION

James E. White
St. Cloud State University

THOMSON
———*———™
WADSWORTH

Australia • Canada • Mexico • Singapore • Spain • United Kingdom • United States

THOMSON
WADSWORTH

Publisher: Holly J. Allen
Philosophy Editor: Steve Wainwright
Assistant Editors: Lee McCracken, Barbara Hillaker
Editorial Assistant: John Gahbauer
Technology Project Manager: Julie Aguilar
Marketing Manager: Worth Hawes
Marketing Assistant: Andrew Keay
Advertising Project Manager: Laurel Anderson
Executive Art Director: Maria Epes
Print/Media Buyer: Lisa Claudeanos

Permissions Editor: Chelsea Junget
Production Service: Matrix Productions
Copy Editor: Cheryl Smith
Cover Designer: Yvo Riezebos
Cover Image: *Ancient Landscape,* 1982,
 by George Dannatt (Getty Images)
Compositor: International Typesetting
 and Composition
Text and Cover Printer: Malloy Incorporated

Printed in the United States of America
1 2 3 4 5 6 7 08 07 06 05 04

For more information about our products, contact us at:
Thomson Learning Academic Resource Center
1-800-423-0563
For permission to use material from this text or product,
submit a request online at **http://www.thomsonrights.com**.
Any additional questions about permissions can be submitted
by email to **thomsonrights@thomson.com**.

Library of Congress Control Number: 2004117547
ISBN 0-534-62584-3

Thomson Wadsworth
10 Davis Drive
Belmont, CA 94002-3098
USA

Asia
Thomson Learning
5 Shenton Way #01-01
UIC Building
Singapore 068808

Australia/New Zealand
Thomson Learning
102 Dodds Street
Southbank, Victoria 3006
Australia

Canada
Nelson
1120 Birchmount Road
Toronto, Ontario M1K 5G4
Canada

Europe/Middle East/Africa
Thomson Learning
High Holborn House
50/51 Bedford Row
London WC1R 4LR
United Kingdom

Latin America
Thomson Learning
Seneca, 53
Colonia Polanco
11560 Mexico D.F.
Mexico

Spain/Portugal
Paraninfo
Calle Magallanes, 25
28015 Madrid, Spain

Contents

Introduction

Factual Background

The history of humans is a sad chronicle of war and terrorism. Thus far there have been no nuclear or biological wars, but almost every year there has been a conventional war or an act of terrorism somewhere in the world. India and Pakistan have been fighting in the disputed area of Kashmir for over fifty years. Israel has fought several wars, and continues to fight the Palestinians on a daily basis. The Palestinians respond with suicide bombers. There was a war in Bosnia generated by ethnic differences. Saddam Hussein invaded Kuwait and the result was the first Gulf War. A short list of wars in the twentieth century includes World Wars I and II, the Korean War, the Vietnam War, and a bitter struggle in Afghanistan when Russian forces tried to invade. Iran and Iraq fought a bloody war, with Iraq being armed and supported by the United States. In 2001, U.S. and British forces attacked Afghanistan in response to the 9/11 terrorist attacks. In 2003, U.S. and British troops invaded and occupied Iraq, claiming that Iraq had weapons of mass destruction and ties to Al Qaeda, the terrorist organization responsible for the 9/11 attacks. In 2004, insurgents in Iraq continued fighting U.S. troops with casualties on both sides, and many innocent civilians were killed. (For more on the invasion and occupation of Iraq, see the first Problem Case.)

Terrorist attacks have dramatically increased in the twenty-first century. Suicide bombings, missile strikes, shootings, and other attacks have become a frequent occurrence in Iraq and Israel. Sometimes soldiers or the police are killed, but many times it is civilians who die. In 2004, Israeli missiles killed Sheik Ahmed Yassin, the spiritual leader of the militant group Hamas, which Israel claimed was responsible for terrorist bombings in Israel. In 2004, ten bombs ripped through four commuter trains in Madrid during the morning rush hour, killing nearly 200 and wounding more than 1,400. This was the deadliest terrorist attack on a European target since World War II. On September 11, 2001, nineteen terrorists hijacked four airplanes. They crashed two of the planes into the World Trade Center in New York City, destroying the twin towers. It is estimated that 3,000 people were killed. A third plane hit the Pentagon, killing nearly 200 workers. The fourth plane crashed in rural southwest Pennsylvania after the passengers overpowered the terrorists. A total of 266 people were killed on the four planes. This was the most devastating terrorist attack in U.S. history. Some compared it to the Japanese attack on Pearl Harbor that resulted in war with Japan, a war that ended shortly after Hiroshima and Nagasaki were destroyed with nuclear bombs in August 1945.

The United States produced convincing evidence that Osama bin Laden and his Al Qaeda network of terrorists were responsible for the 9/11 attacks. On September 23, 2001, bin Laden issued a statement urging his followers to remain steadfast on the path of jihad against the infidels, that is, the United States and her allies. In 2004, bin Laden had still not been captured, and he continued to issue videos declaring war against the infidels.

This was only the latest and most shocking of a series of terrorist attacks on U.S. citizens and servicemen. On October 12, 2000, a terrorist bombing killed seventeen U.S. sailors aboard the U.S.S. Cole as it refueled in Yemen's port of Aden. The United States said that bin Laden was the prime suspect. On August 7, 1998, there were car bombings of U.S. embassies in Nairobi, Kenya, and Dar es Salaam, Tanzania. More than 5,500 people were injured and 224 were killed. Once again the prime suspect was Osama bin Laden. In June, 1996, a truck bomb exploded outside the Khobar Towers in Dharan, Saudi Arabia, killing 19 U.S. servicemen and wounding hundreds of other people. Members of a radical Lebanese terrorist group, Hizballah, were indicted for the attack. On February 26, 1993, a bomb exploded in a parking garage below the World Trade Center, killing 6 people and wounding more than 1,000. Six radical Muslim terrorists were convicted and sentenced to life in prison. On April 19, 1995, a federal building in Oklahoma City was destroyed by a truck bomb. There were 168 deaths. Timothy J. McVeigh was executed for the attack and Terry L. Nichols was sentenced to life in prison. On December 21, 1998, Pam Am flight 103 exploded over Lockerbie, Scotland, killing 270 people onboard. Two Libyan intelligence officers were accused of planting a suitcase containing the bomb. One was convicted in February 2001 and the other was set free.

The Readings

A traditional and important position on war and terrorism is pacifism. Pacifism can take different forms. In the first reading for the chapter, Lackey distinguishes between four different types of pacifism: (1) the view that all killing is wrong, (2) the view that all violence is wrong, (3) the view that personal violence is always wrong, but political violence is sometimes morally right, and (4) the view that personal violence is sometimes morally permissible, but war is always morally wrong. Albert Schweitzer's position is an example of the first type of pacifism; he held that all killing is wrong because all life is sacred. Mohandas Gandhi's pacifism is an example of the second type because he opposed all violence. According to Lackey, a problem with both of these views is that sometimes killing or violence is required to save lives. For example, shouldn't a terrorist airplane hijacker be killed or restrained to prevent the hijacker from crashing the plane and killing all the passengers? The third view that condemns personal violence but allows political violence is attributed to St. Augustine. But this view has a problem with personal self-defense. Most people would agree that personal violence is justified in defense of one's life, as in the case of the terrorist airplane hijacker. The kind of pacifism that Lackey supports is the fourth view, which condemns all war as morally wrong but allows some personal violence. But this antiwar pacifism has a problem, too. Why can't some wars be justified by appealing to some great moral good such as political freedom? Certainly the Revolutionary War in America (to use Lackey's own example) is defended in this way.

Another important view on war is just war theory. Medieval Christian theologians called Scholastics originally formulated the theory, and it has been discussed ever since. The theory distinguishes between two questions about war. First, there is the question about the right to go to war, called *jus ad bellum,* or "right to war": What are the conditions that justify going to war? Second, there is the question about the right conduct in war, called *jus in bello,* or "right in war": How should combatants conduct themselves in fighting a war?

As O'Brien explains it in the second reading, then, just war theory has two components, one concerned with the right to go to war and the other with the conduct of war. Three main conditions have to be met to establish the right to go to war: (1) the war must be declared by a competent authority, (2) there must be a just cause, and (3) there must be a right intention that ultimately aims at peace. The just cause condition is subdivided into four more conditions: the substance of the just cause, the form of the just cause, the proportionality of ends and means, and the requirement of the exhaustion of peaceful remedies. The substance of the just cause is the reason for going to war, such as "to protect the innocent from unjust attack." This reason could be given to justify going to war against Germany in World War II. The form of the just cause is either defensive or offensive. Defensive wars are easier to justify than offensive ones. O'Brien notes, however, that offensive wars of vindictive justice against infidels or heretics were once permitted. (As we shall see, this is similar to the doctrine of jihad.) The requirement of proportionality has to do with general means and ends; basically the idea is that the ultimate end, such as political freedom or a democratic society, must be sufficiently good to justify the evil of warfare. (Khatchadourian in the third reading calls this the political principle of proportionality.) The fourth requirement is that going to war should be a last resort after all peaceful remedies, such as negotiation, mediation, and arbitration, have failed.

Two basic principles limit conduct in a just war, the principle of proportion and the principle of discrimination. The principle of proportion says that the intermediate military ends, such as the capture of an enemy position, must justify the means used, such as the firing of rockets. (Khatchadourian calls this the military principle of proportionality.) The principle of discrimination prohibits intentional attacks on noncombatants and nonmilitary targets. This principle is the subject of much debate, as we will see.

In the third reading, Khatchadourian applies just war theory to terrorism. He argues that all forms of terrorism (predatory, retaliatory, political, and moral/religious) are always wrong because they flagrantly violate the principles of just war theory and they violate basic human rights. They also violate the principle of necessity that forbids the wanton destruction of life and property. (O'Brien discusses this principle as one of the applications of the military principle of proportionality.) They violate the principle of discrimination because innocent people are killed or harmed. (Khatchodourian condemns the tendency of political, retaliatory, or moralistic terrorists to baselessly enlarge the circle of allegedly noninnocent people.) Acts of terrorism also violate the principle of proportion in both its political form applying to the right to go to war and its military form applying to the conduct of war. All but the moral/religious type violate a further condition of just war theory, the condition of a just cause. Finally, Khatchadourian argues that all forms of terrorism violate the fundamental human rights of the victims, including the right to autonomy, the negative right to life, and the right to be treated as a moral person.

In the fourth reading, Calhoun also applies just war theory to terrorism, but with different results than Khatchadourian's. Her focus is on political and moral/religious terrorists. Unlike Khatchadourian, she does not try to show that terrorist acts are wrong. Instead she wants to show how just war theory can be used by terrorists to defend their actions, at least to themselves and their followers, using the very same theory that democratic nations use to justify their military campaigns. Terrorists who do this see themselves as fighting a "just war." To see how they can do this, we need to look more closely at just war theory, and particularly the doctrine of double effect. How can a nation justify dropping bombs on another nation when this act results in the killing of innocent civilians? If the principle of discrimination is understood as absolutely forbidding killing innocents, then no modern war could be justified. O'Brien and Lackey both make this point in the readings. To justify killing innocents, just war theorists appeal to the Catholic doctrine of double effect. The doctrine distinguishes between two effects of an action, an intended effect and one that is foreseen but not intended, a side effect. The doctrine says that as long as the intended consequence of an act is good (for example, winning a war or relief of suffering), then a bad foreseen consequence (for example, the death of innocents) is morally allowed, provided this bad consequence is not intended. Calhoun argues that terrorists can use this sort of reasoning to justify their actions, as Timothy McVeigh did when he characterized the deaths of innocent people in the Oklahoma City bombing as " collateral damage." In other words, she argues, "just war" rationalizations are available to everyone, bin Laden as well as President Bush. Terrorists can present themselves to their followers as warriors for justice, and not as mere murderers or vigilantes.

In the fifth reading, Luban discusses the new War on Terrorism, which is the result of the 9/11 attacks. According to Luban, the current fight against terrorism does not fit the traditional model of war. Instead it uses a new hybrid war-law model that combines features of the war model with a law model. The new war model allows the use of lethal force, the foreseen but unintended killing of innocents, and the capturing and killing of suspected terrorists. These are features of war. But in traditional war, the enemy can legitimately fight back, other nations can opt for neutrality, and enemy soldiers have certain rights under the Geneva Convention. The War on Terrorism rejects these features by appealing to a law model. Terrorists are criminals so they cannot legitimately fight back. Other nations cannot be neutral when it comes to illegal murder. If they harbor or aid terrorists, they are against us. Finally, terrorists are treated as enemy combatants rather than soldiers or ordinary criminals, and as such they have no rights, neither the rights of ordinary criminals nor the rights of soldiers under the Geneva Convention. There is no presumption of innocence, no right to a hearing, and they can be detained indefinitely. Even torture is allowable. So according to Luban, the War on Terrorism produces an end of international human rights because anyone identified as a terrorist has no rights. (For an example of the treatment of suspected terrorists, see the case of Jose Padilla in the Problem Cases.)

Pacifism and just war theory have dominated discussion of war and terrorism in Western thought. Both of these positions developed in the tradition of Christianity. But there is another important doctrine about war that comes from Islam and is used to justify both terrorism and war. This is the Islamic doctrine of jihad.

Although the term "jihad" is often translated as "holy war," Knapp in the last reading says that this is not exactly what the term means. Literally it means struggle or striving in the path of God for a noble cause. Knapp discusses the classic and modern doctrine of jihad as it is applied to warfare. The classic view of jihad allowed defensive war against enemies of Islam, but it did not sanction the killing of all non-Muslims or even their conversion by force. He quotes the Koran (2:256): "There is no compulsion in religion." Killing of other Muslims could only be justified by classifying them as non-Muslims, e.g., as apostates or rebels. He notes that the Islamic law tradition was very hostile toward terrorism and severely punished rebels who attacked innocent victims. Modern Islamic militants have changed the doctrine of jihad. They see themselves as fighting to restore land and nations lost to Islam. The Palestinians are fighting to regain the land taken away from them by Isarel. Osama bin Laden claims that Americans are infidels occupying holy places in Saudi Arabia, namely the cities of Mecca and Medina, and fighting a war of annihiliation against Iraq, which for 500 years was the heart of an Islamic empire. But according to Knapp, the classic and modern doctrines of jihad do not condone indiscriminate killing or terrorism as practiced by suicide bombers or Al Qaeda. The Islamic militants have hijacked the doctrine of jihad to serve their own purposes.

Philosophical Issues

The readings in the chapter raise some very important issues. Can war be justified, and if so, how? Pacifists such as Schweitzer and Gandhi, who were opposed to all killing or all violence, hold that no war is ever justified. The problem with these absolutist views is that there seems to be an obvious exception, namely, killing or violence in the defense of one's life. Lackey's antiwar pacifism is not so easily dismissed. If one agrees that the killing of soldiers and civilians is a very great evil, one that cannot be balanced by goods such as political freedom, then it seems very difficult, if not impossible, to justify modern wars.

Just war theorists such as O'Brien try to justify modern wars such as World War II, but to do so they have to modify or interpret the principles of the theory. The most troublesome principle is the one about discrimination. As O'Brien says, if this principle is understood to forbid absolutely the killing of noncombatants, then it is hard to see how any modern war could be justified, since they all involved killing noncombatants. Perhaps the most graphic example was the atomic bombing of Hiroshima and Nagasaki, which killed over 200,000 innocent noncombatants. There are various ways to get around the problem. One is to deny that there are any innocent noncombatants in war; everyone in an enemy nation is a legitimate target. (Some terrorists take this position, too.) The most common way of justifying the killing of innocents, as we have seen, is to appeal to the Catholic doctrine of double effect.

There is debate about how to formulate and apply the doctrine of double effect. In the reading, O'Brien admits that the distinction between the two effects, one that is directly intended and the other, an unintended side effect, is often difficult to accept. Consider President Harry Truman's decision to bomb Hiroshima and Nagasaki. At the time, he said that his decision was based on the fact that an invasion of Japan would cost the lives of thousands of American soldiers, and he wanted to save those lives. But he surely knew that using atomic bombs on these unde-fended cities would result in the deaths of thousands of innocent Japanese noncom-batants. Did he directly intend the killing of innocents or merely foresee this killing as an unintended consequence? Can we make the distinction in this case, and if we do, then what is the basis for the distinction?

Are acts of terrorism ever justified? As we have seen, Khatchadourian does not think so, and most pacifists would agree, with the possible exception of pacifists who forbid personal violence but allow political violence. Calhoun argues that terrorists can and do appeal to the just war theory, the very theory that Khatchadourian uses to demonstrate that terrorism is always wrong. How can just war theory be used to defend terrorism? Calhoun argues that terrorists can appeal to the doctrine of dou-ble effect. To see how this might be done, let's take another look at the doctrine as stated by Father Richard McCormick and quoted by O'Brien. McCormick says, "It is immoral directly to take innocent human life except with divine authorization." Why is the killing of innocents allowed if there is divine authorization? One explana-tion is that just war theory was developed by Catholic theologians to defend the holy crusades against infidels, crusades that they were believed to be commanded by God. But of course fundamentalist Muslim terrorists also believe they have divine authorization; they believe they are engaged in a holy war commanded by Allah against infidels. Thus both Christians and Muslims claim divine authorization for war and terrorism.

Now let us turn to the distinction between direct and indirect killing, which is at the heart of the doctrine of double effect. As McCormick explains it, "Direct taking of human life implies that one performs a lethal action with the intention that death should result for himself or another. Death is therefore deliberately willed as the effect of one's action." But Muslim terrorists may sincerely believe that all things happen by Allah's will, and they do not will anything, much less the death of others. They are merely submitting to the will of Allah, and Allah commands them to jihad. So they can claim that the deaths that result from their actions are not positively willed, but merely foreseen as a consequence of following Allah's commands. In other words, they are only indirectly killing innocents. It appears, then, that terror-ists can attempt to justify their actions by appealing to the Catholic doctrine of dou-ble effect, at least as it is stated by McCormick.

How do we define terrorism? This is another issue discussed in the readings. Calhoun argues that there is no satisfactory definition of terrorism. The moral defi-nition, which defines terrorism as killing or threatening to kill innocent people, is unsatisfactory because it seems to apply to every nation that has engaged in bomb-ing campaigns resulting in the deaths of innocent children. The legal definition, which defines terrorism as illegal acts of killing or harming people, is defective because it would not apply to the reign of terror imposed by the Third Reich in Nazi Germany. Khatchadourian also rejects moral definitions that make terrorism wrong by definition, and he agrees that essentialist definitions of terrorism are inad-equate. They are either too broad or too narrow. Nevertheless, Khatchadourian thinks that the vague and contested word terrorism has a core meaning that includes the idea that terrorist acts are acts of coercion or force aiming at monetary gain, revenge, a political end, or a moral/religious end. Also, he says, terrorism has a bifocal character that distinguishes it from other forms of coercion or force. That is, terrorism not only aims at killing or harming victims, it also aims at producing fear and terror in the victimized, those who are the indirect but real targets of terrorist acts.

Finally, how do we deal with terrorists? This is an issue raised by Luban. Do we treat them as enemy soldiers that have rights under the Geneva Convention, e.g., the right not to be tortured, the right to be fed, clothed, given medical treatment, and released when hostilities are over? Or are they to be considered criminals? If so, do they have the legal rights of ordinary criminals such as the presumption of innocence, the right to a trial, the right to be defended by a lawyer, the right to not testify against themselves, and the right to not be held without charges? Or are they enemy combatants who have neither the rights of soldiers nor ordinary criminals?

Pacifism

DOUGLAS P. LACKEY

Douglas P. Lackey is professor of philosophy at Baruch College and the Graduate Center of the City University of New York. He is the author of *Moral Principles and Nuclear Weapons* (1984), *Ethics and Strategic Defense: American Philosophers Debate Star Wars and the Future of Nuclear Deterrence* (1989), and *God, Immortality, Ethics: A Concise Introduction to Philosophy* (1990). Our reading is taken from *The Ethics of War and Peace* (1989).

Lackey distinguishes between four types of pacifism. There is the universal pacifist view that all killing is wrong, the universal pacifist view that all violence is wrong, private pacifism that condemns personal violence but not political violence, and antiwar pacifism that allows personal violence but condemns all wars. Lackey discusses objections to all of these views, but he seems to defend antiwar pacifism. Or at least he answers every objection to antiwar pacifism, leaving the reader with the impression that he supports this view.

1. VARIETIES OF PACIFISM

EVERYONE HAS A VAGUE IDEA of what a pacifist is, but few realize that there are many kinds of pacifists. (Sometimes the different kinds quarrel with each other!) One task for the student of

Source: Douglas P. Lackey, "Pacifism" from *The Ethics of War and Peace* by Douglas P. Lackey, pp. 6–24. Prentice Hall, Inc. Copyright 1989. Reprinted by permission of Pearson Education, Inc., Upper Saddle River, NJ.

international ethics is to distinguish the different types of pacifism and to identify which types represent genuine moral theories.

Most of us at some time or other have run into the "live and let live" pacifist, the person who says, "I am absolutely opposed to killing and violence—but I don't seek to impose my own code on anyone else. If other people want to use violence, so be it. They have their values and I have mine." For such a person, pacifism is one life style among others, a life style committed to gentleness and care, and opposed to belligerence and militarism. Doubtless, many people who express such commitments are sincere and are prepared to live by their beliefs. At the same time, it is important to see why "live and let live" pacifism does not constitute a moral point of view.

When someone judges that a certain action, A, is morally wrong, that judgment entails that no one should do A. Thus, there is no way to have moral values without believing that these values apply to other people. If a person says that A is morally wrong but that it doesn't matter if other people do A, than that person either is being inconsistent or doesn't know what the word "moral" means. If a person believes that killing, in certain circumstances, is morally wrong, that belief implies that no one should kill, at least in those circumstances. If a pacifist claims that killing is wrong in *all* circumstances, but that it is permissible for other people to kill on occasion, then he has not understood the universal character of genuine moral principles. If pacifism is to be a moral theory, it must be prescribed for all or prescribed for none.

Once one recognizes this "universalizing" character of genuine moral beliefs, one will take moral commitments more seriously than those who treat a moral code as a personal life-style. Since moral principles apply to everyone, we must take care that our moral principles are correct, checking that they are not inconsistent with each other, developing and adjusting them so that they are detailed and subtle enough to deal with a variety of circumstances, and making sure that they are defensible against the objections of those who do not accept them. Of course many pacifists do take the business of morality seriously and advance pacifism as a genuine moral position, not as a mere life-style. All such serious pacifists believe that *everyone* ought to be a pacifist, and that those who reject pacifism are deluded or wicked. Moreover, they do not simply endorse pacifism; they offer arguments in its defense.

We will consider four types of pacifist moral theory. First, there are pacifists who maintain that the central idea of pacifism is the immorality of killing. Second, there are pacifists who maintain that the essence of pacifism is the immorality of violence, whether this be violence in personal relations or violence in relations between nation-states. Third, there are pacifists who argue that personal violence is always morally wrong but that political violence is sometimes morally right: for example, that it is sometimes morally permissible for a nation to go to war. Fourth and finally, there are pacifists who believe that personal violence is sometimes permissible but that war is always morally wrong.

Albert Schweitzer, who opposed all killing on the grounds that life is sacred, was the first sort of pacifist. Mohandas Gandhi and Leo Tolstoy, who opposed not only killing but every kind of coercion and violence, were pacifists of the second sort: I will call such pacifists "universal pacifists." St. Augustine, who condemned self-defense but endorsed wars against heretics, was a pacifist of the third sort. Let us call him a "private pacifist," since he condemned only violence in the private sphere. Pacifists of the fourth sort, increasingly common in the modern era of nuclear and total war, I will call "antiwar pacifists."

2. THE PROHIBITION AGAINST KILLING

(a) The Biblical Prohibition

One simple and common argument for pacifism is the argument that the Bible, God's revealed word, says to all people "Thou shalt not kill" (Exod. 20:13). Some pacifists interpret this sentence as implying that no one should kill under any circumstances, unless God indicates that this command is suspended, as He did when He commanded Abraham to slay Isaac. The justification for this interpretation is the words themselves, "Thou shalt not kill," which are presented in the Bible bluntly and without qualification, not only in Exodus but also in Deuteronomy (5:17).

This argument, however, is subject to a great many criticisms. The original language of Exodus and Deuteronomy is Hebrew, and the consensus of scholarship says that the Hebrew sentence at Exodus 20:23, "Lo Tirzach," is best translated as "Thou shalt do no murder," not as "Thou shalt not kill." If this translation is correct, then Exodus 20:13 does not forbid all killing but only those killings that happen to be murders. Furthermore, there are many places in the Bible where God commands human beings to kill in specified circumstances. God announces 613 commandments in all, and these include "Thou shalt not suffer a witch to live" (Exod. 22:18); "He that blasphemeth the name of the Lord . . . shall surely be put to death, and all the congregation shall stone him" (Lev. 24:16); "He that killeth any man shall surely be put to death" (Lev. 24:17); and so forth. It is difficult to argue that these instructions are like God's specific instructions to Abraham to slay Isaac: these are general commandments to be applied by many people, to many people, day in and day out. They are at least as general and as divinely sanctioned as the commandment translated "Thou shalt not kill."

There are other difficulties for pacifists who pin their hopes on prohibitions in the Hebrew Bible. Even if the commandment "Thou shalt not kill," properly interpreted, did prohibit all types of killing, the skeptics can ask whether this, by itself, proves that all killing is immoral. First, how do we know that statements in the Hebrew Bible really are God's word, and not just the guesses of ancient scribes? Second, even if the commandments in the Bible do express God's views, why are we morally bound to obey divine commands? (To say that we will be punished if we do not obey is to appeal to fear and self-interest, not to moral sentiments). Third, are the commandments in the Old Testament laws for all people, or just laws for the children of Israel? If they are laws for all people, then all people who do not eat unleavened bread for Passover are either deluded or wicked. If they are laws only for the children of Israel, they are religious laws and not moral laws, since they lack the universality that all moral laws must have.

Finally, the argument assumes the existence of God, and philosophers report that the existence of God is not easy to demonstrate. Even many religious believers are more confident of the truth of basic moral judgments, such as "Small children should not be tortured to death for purposes of amusement," than they are confident of the existence of God. For such people, it would seem odd to try to justify moral principles by appeals to religious principles, since the evidence for those religious principles is weaker than the evidence for the moral principles they are supposed to justify.

(b) The Sacredness of Life

There are, however, people who oppose all killing but do not seek justification in divine revelation. Many of these defend pacifism by appeal to the sacredness of life. Almost everyone is struck with wonder when watching the movements and reactions of a newborn baby, and almost everyone can be provoked to awe by the study of living things, great and small. The complexity of the mechanisms found in living bodies, combined with the efficiency with which they fulfill their functions, is not matched by any of the processes in nonliving matter. People who are particularly awestruck by the beauty of living things infer these feelings that life is sacred, that all killing is wrong.

Different versions of pacifism have been derived from beliefs about the sacredness of life. The most extreme version forbids the killing of any living thing. This view was allegedly held by Pythagoras, and presently held by members of the Jain religion in India. (Those who think that such pacifists must soon starve to death should note that a life-sustaining diet can easily be constructed from milk, honey, fallen fruit and vegetables, and other items that are consumable without prior killing.) A less extreme view sanctions the killing of plants but forbids the killing of animals. The most moderate view prohibits only the killing of fellow beings.

There is deep appeal in an argument that connects the sacredness of life with the wrongfulness of taking life. Even people who are not pacifists are often revolted by the spectacle of killing, and most Americans would be unable to eat meat if they had to watch how the animals whose flesh they consume had been slaughtered, or if they had to do the slaughtering themselves. Most people sense that they do not own the world they inhabit and recognize that they are not free to do with the world as they will, that the things in it, most especially living things, are worthy of respect and care. Seemingly nothing could violate the respect living things deserve more than killing, especially since much of the taking of human and nonhuman life is so obviously unnecessary.

But with the introduction of the word "unnecessary" a paradox arises. Sometimes—less often that we think, but sometimes—the taking of some lives will save other lives. Does the principle that life is sacred and ought to be preserved imply that nothing should ever be killed, or does it imply that as much life should be preserved as possible? Obviously pacifists take the former view; nonpacifists, the latter.

The view that killing is wrong because it destroys what is sacred seems to imply that killing is wrong because killing diminishes the amount of good in the world. It seems to follow that if a person can save more lives by killing than by refusing to kill, arguments about the sacredness of life would not show that killing in these circumstances is wrong. (It might be wrong for other reasons.) The more lives saved, the greater the quantity of good in the world.

The difficulty that some killing might, on balance, save lives, is not the only problem for pacifism based on the sacredness of life. If preserving life is the highest value, a value not comparable with other, non-life-preserving goods, it follows that any acts which place life at risk are immoral. But many admirable actions have been undertaken in the face of death, and many less heroic but morally impeccable actions—driving on a road at moderate speed, authorizing a commercial flight to take off, and so forth—place life at risk. In cases of martyrdom in which

people choose death over religious conversion, life is just as much destroyed as it is in a common murder. Yet, on the whole, automobile drivers, air traffic controllers, and religious martyrs are not thought to be wicked. Likewise, people on life-sustaining machinery sometimes request that the machines be turned off, on the grounds that quality of life matters more than quantity of life. We may consider such people mistaken, but we hardly think that they are morally depraved.

In answering this objection, the pacifist may wish to distinguish between *killing other people* and *getting oneself killed,* arguing that only the former is immoral. But although there is a genuine distinction between killing and getting killed, the distinction does not entail that killing other people destroys life but getting oneself killed does not. If life is sacred, life, including one's own life, must be preserved at all cost. In many cases, people consider the price of preserving their own lives simply too high.

(c) The Right to Life

Some pacifists may try to avoid the difficulties of the "sacredness of life" view by arguing that the essential immorality of killing is that it violates the *right to life* that every human being possesses. If people have a right to life, then it is never morally permissible to kill some people in order to save others, since according to the usual interpretation of rights, it is never permissible to violate a right in order to secure some good.

A discussion of the logic of rights in general and the right to life in particular is beyond the scope of this book. But a number of students of this subject are prepared to argue that the possession of any right implies the permissibility of defending that right against aggression: if this were not so, what would be the point of asserting the existence of rights? But if the possession of a right to life implies the permissibility of defending that right against aggression—a defense that may require killing the aggressor—then the existence of a right to life cannot by itself imply the impermissiblity of killing. On this view, the right to life implies the right to self-defense, including violent self-defense. It does not imply pacifism.

3. UNIVERSAL PACIFISM

(a) Christian Pacifism

Universal pacifists are morally opposed to all violence, not just to killing. Many universal pacifists derive their views from the Christian Gospels. In the Sermon on the Mount, Christ taught:

> Ye have heard that it hath been said, An eye for an eye, a tooth for a tooth:
>
> But I say unto you, that ye resist not evil: but whosoever shall smite thee on the right cheek, turn to him the other also. . . .
>
> Ye have heard it said, thou shalt love thy neighbor, and hate thine enemy. But I say unto you, Love your enemies, bless them that curse you, do good to them that hate you. . . . that ye may be the children of your father which is in heaven: for he maketh the sun to rise on the evil and on the good, and sendeth the rain on the just and the unjust. (Matt, 5:38–45)

In the early centuries of the Christian era, it was widely assumed that to follow Christ and to obey His teaching meant that one should reject violence and refuse service in the Roman army. But by the fifth century, after the Roman Empire had become Christian and after barbarian Goths in 410 sacked Rome itself, Church Fathers debated whether Christ really intended that the Empire and its Church should remain undefended. The Church Fathers noticed passages in the Gospels that seem to contradict pacifism:

> Think not that I am come to send peace on earth: I came not to send peace, but a sword.
>
> For I am come to set a man at variance against his father, and the daughter against her mother, and the daughter-in-law against her mother-in-law. (Matt. 10:34–35)

And there are several instances in the Gospels (for instance, Matt. 8:5–10) in which Jesus encounters soldiers and does not rebuke them for engaging in an occupation that is essentially committed to violence. Rather, he argues, "Render unto Caesar the things which are Caesar's; and unto God the things that are God's" (Matt. 22:21). This would seem to include military service, or at least taxes to pay for the army.

A thorough analysis of whether the Gospels command pacifism is beyond the scope of this book. The passages in the Sermon on the Mount seem to be clearly pacifist; yet many eminent scholars have denied the pacifist message. A more interesting question, for philosophy, if not for biblical scholarship, is this: If Jesus did preach pacifism in the Sermon on the Mount, did He preach it as a *moral* doctrine?

Jesus did not view his teaching as replacing the moral law as he knew it:

> Think not that I am come to destroy the law, or the prophets: I am come not to destroy, but to fulfill. . . .
>
> Till heaven and earth pass, one jot or one tittle shall in no wise pass from the law, till all be fulfilled. (Matt. 5:17–18)

Perhaps, then, the prescriptions of the Sermon on the Mount should be interpreted as rules that one must obey in order to follow Christ, or rules that one must follow in order to obtain salvation. But it does not follow from this alone that everyone has an obligation to follow Christ, and it does not follow from this alone that everyone has an obligation to seek salvation. Even Christians will admit that some people have refused to become Christians and have led morally admirable lives nonetheless; and if salvation is a good, one can nevertheless choose to reject it, just as a citizen can neglect to hand in a winning lottery ticket without breaking the law. If so, the prescriptions of the Sermon on the Mount apply only to Christians seeking a Christian salvation. They are not universally binding rules and do not qualify as moral principles.

(b) The Moral Exemplar Argument

Many people and at least one illustrious philosopher, Immanuel Kant, believe that morally proper action consists in choosing to act in such a way that your conduct could serve as an example for all mankind. (It was Kant's genius to recognize that moral conduct is *essentially* exemplary.) Some universal pacifists appeal to this idea, arguing that if everyone were a pacifist, the world would be a much better place than it is now. This is an argument that Leo Tolstoy (1828–1910) used to support the Gospel prescription not to resist evil:

> [Christ] put the proposition of non-resistance to evil is such a way that, according to his teaching, it was to be the foundation of the joint life of men and was to free humanity from the evil that is inflicted on itself. (*My Religion,* Ch. 4) Instead of having the whole life based on violence and every joy obtained and guarded through violence; instead of seeing each one of us punished or inflicting punishment from childhood to old age, I imagined that we were all impressed in word and deed by the idea that vengeance is a very low, animal feeling; that violence is not only a disgraceful act, but also one that deprives man of true happiness. . . .
>
> I imagined that instead of those national hatreds which are impressed on us under the form of patriotism, instead of those glorifications of murder, called wars . . . that we were impressed with the idea that the recognition of any countries, special laws, borders, lands, is a sign of grossest ignorance. . . .
>
> Through the fulfillment of these commandments, the life of men will be what every human heart seeks and desires. All men will be brothers and everybody will always be at peace with others, enjoying all the benefits of the world. (*My Religion,* Ch. 6)

Few would deny that if everyone were a pacifist, the world would be a better place, perhaps even a paradise. Furthermore, since the argument is essentially hypothetical, it cannot be refuted (as many nonpacifists believe) by pointing out that not everyone will become a pacifist. The problem is whether this argument can establish pacifism as a moral imperative.

One difficulty with the argument is that it seems to rely on a premise the truth of which is purely verbal. In what way would the world be a

better place if people gave up fighting? The most obvious way is that the world would be better because there would be no war. But the statement "If everyone gave up fighting, there would be no war" is true by definition, since "war" implies "fighting." It is difficult to see how a statement that simply relates the meanings of words could tell us something about our moral obligations.

A deeper problem with Tolstoy's argument is that "resist not evil" is not the only rule that would yield paradise if everyone obeyed it. Suppose that everyone in the world subscribed to the principle "Use violence, but only in self-defense." If everyone used violence only in self-defense, the same consequences would follow as would arise from universal acceptance of the rule "Never use violence." Consequently, pacifism cannot be shown to be superior to nonpacifism by noting the good consequences that would undeniably ensue if everyone were a pacifist.

(c) Gandhian Pacifism

Certainly the most interesting and effective pacifist of the twentieth century was Mohandas Gandhi (1869–1948). Though a devout Hindu, Gandhi developed his doctrine of nonviolence from elementary metaphysical concepts that are by no means special to Hinduism:

> Man as an animal is violent spirit is nt but as on-violent. The moment he awakes to the spirit he cannot remain violent. Either he progresses towards *ahimsa* [nonviolence] or rushes to his doom. (*Nonviolence in Peace and War,* I, p. 311)

The requirement not to be violent seems wholly negative; sleeping people achieve it with ease. But for Gandhi the essential moral task is not merely to be nonviolent but to use the force of the soul (*satyagraha,* "truth grasping") in a continual struggle for justice. The methods of applied *satyagraha* developed by Gandhi—the weaponless marches, the sit-downs and sit-ins, strikes and boycotts, fasts and prayers—captured the admiration of the world and have been widely copied, most notably by Martin Luther King, Jr., in his campaigns against racial discrimination. According to Gandhi, each person, by engaging in *satyagraha* and experiencing suffering on behalf of justice, purifies the soul from pollution emanating from man's animal nature:

> A *satyagrahi* is dead to his body even before his enemy attempts to kill him, i.e. he is free from the attachments of his body and lives only in the victory of his soul. (*Nonviolence in Peace and War*, I, p. 318) Nonviolence implies as complete self-purification as is humanly possible. (*Nonviolence in Peace and War*, I, p. 111)

By acting nonviolently, pacifists not only purify their own souls but also transform the souls of their opponents: "A nonviolent revolution is not a program of seizure of power. It is a program of transformation of relationships, ending in peaceful transfer of power" (*Nonviolence in Peace and War*, II, p. 8)

Though in most places Gandhi emphasizes the personal redemption that is possible only through nonviolent resistance to evil, the spiritually positive effect of nonviolence on evil opponents is perhaps equally important, since "The soul of the *satagrahi* is love" (*Nonviolence in Peace and War*, II, p. 59).

Gandhi, then, is far from preaching the sacredness of biological life. What matters is not biological life but the condition of the soul, the natural and proper state of which is *ahimsa*. The evil of violence is that it distorts and disrupts this natural condition of the soul. The basic moral law (*dharma*) for all people is to seek the restoration of their souls to the harmony of *ahimsa*. This spiritual restoration cannot be achieved by violence, but only by the application of *satyagraha*. Disharmony cannot produce harmony; violence cannot produce spiritual peace.

The "sacredness of life" defense of pacifism ran into difficulties analyzing situations in which taking one life could save many lives. For Gandhi, this is no problem at all: taking one life may save many biological lives, but it will not save souls. On the contrary, the soul of the killer will be perverted by the act, and that perversion—not the loss of life—is what matters morally.

The system of values professed by Gandhi—that the highest human good is a harmonious condition of soul—must be kept in mind when considering the frequent accusation that Gandhi's method of nonviolent resistance "does not work," that nonviolence alone did not and could not force the British to leave India, and that nonviolent resistance to murderous tyrants like Hitler will only provoke the mass murder of the innocent. Perhaps the practice of nonviolence could not "defeat" the British or "defeat" Hitler, but by Gandhi's standard the use of military force would only produce a greater defeat, perverting the souls of thousands engaged in war and intensifying the will to violence on the opposing side. On the other hand, the soul of the *satyagrahi* will be strengthened and purified by nonviolent struggle against British imperialism or German Nazism, and in this purification the Gandhian pacifist can obtain spiritual victory even in the face of political defeat.

India did not adopt the creed of nonviolence after the British left in 1948, and it is hardly likely that any modern nation-state will organize its international affairs along Gandhian lines. But none of this affects the validity of Gandhi's arguments, which indicate how things ought to be, not how they are. We have seen that Gandhi's principles do not falter in the face of situations in which taking one life can save lives on balance. But what of situations in which the sacrifice of spiritual purity by one will prevent the corruption of many souls? Suppose, for example, that a Gandhian believes (on good evidence) that a well-timed commando raid will prevent a nation from embarking on an aggressive war, a war that would inflame whole populations with hatred for the enemy. Wouldn't a concern with one's own spiritual purity in such a situation show an immoral lack of concern for the souls of one's fellow men?

Another problem for Gandhi concerns the relationship between violence and coercion. To coerce people is to make them act against their will, for fear of the consequences they will suffer if they do not obey. Coercion, then, is a kind of spiritual violence, directed against the imagination and will of the victim. The "violence" most conspicuously rejected by Gandhi—pushing, shoving, striking with hands, the use of weapons, the placing of bombs and explosives—is essentially physical violence, directed against the bodies of opponents. But if physical violence against bodies is spiritually corrupting, psychological violence directed at the will of opponents must be even more corrupting.

In his writings Gandhi condemned coercion. Yet in practice he can hardly be said to have renounced *psychological* coercion. Obviously he would have preferred to have the British depart from India of their own free will, deciding that it was in their own best interest, or at least morally necessary, to leave. But if the British had decided, in the absence of coercion, to stay, Gandhi was prepared to exert every kind of nonviolent pressure to make them go. And when Gandhi on occasion attempted to achieve political objectives by a "fast unto death," his threat of self-starvation brought enormous psychological pressure on the authorities, who, among other things, feared the riots would ensue should Gandhi die.

The Gandhian pacifist, then, must explain why psychological pressure is permissible if physical pressure is forbidden. One possible answer is that physical pressure cannot transform the soul of the opponents, but psychological pressure, since it operates on the mind, can effect a spiritual transformation. Indeed, Gandhi characterized his terrifying fasts as acts of education, not coercion. But the claim that these fasts were not coercive confuses the noncoercive intention behind the act with its predictable coercive effects; and if education is the name of the game, the nonpacifists will remark that violence has been known to teach a few good lessons in its day. In many spiritual traditions, what matters essentially is not the kind of pressure but that the right pressure be applied at the right time and in the right way. Zen masters have brought students to enlightenment by clouting them on the ears,

and God helped St. Paul to see the light by knocking him off his horse.

In addition to these technical problems, many people will be inclined to reject the system of values from which Gandhi's deductions flow. Many will concede that good character is important and that helping others to develop moral virtues is an important task. But few agree with Gandhi that the development of moral purity is the supreme human good, and that other goods, like the preservation of human life, or progress in the arts and sciences, have little or no value in comparison. If even a little value is conceded to these other things, then on occasion it will be necessary to put aside the project of developing spiritual purity in order to preserve other values. These acts of preservation may require physical violence, and those who use violence to defend life or beauty or liberty may indeed be corrupting their souls. But it is hard to believe that an occasional and necessary act of violence on behalf of these values will totally and permanently corrupt the soul, and those who use violence judiciously may be right in thinking that the saving of life or beauty or liberty may be worth a small or temporary spiritual loss.

4. PRIVATE PACIFISM

Perhaps the rarest form of pacifist is the pacifist who renounces violence in personal relations but condones the use of force in the political sphere. Such a pacifist will not use violence for self-defense but believes that it is permissible for the state to use judicial force against criminals and military force against foreign enemies. A private pacifist renounces self-defense but supports national defense.

(a) Augustine's Limited Pacifism

Historically, private pacifism developed as an attempt to reconcile the demands of the Sermon on the Mount with the Christian duty to charity. The Sermon on the Mount requires Christians to "resist not evil"; the duty of charity requires pity for the weak who suffer the injustice of the strong. For St. Augustine (354–430), one essential message of the Gospels is the good news that this present life is as nothing compared with the life to come. The person who tries to hold on to earthly possessions is deluded as to what is truly valuable: "If any man will sue thee at the law, and take away thy coat, let him have thy cloak also" (Matt. 5:40). What goes for earthly coats should go for earthly life as well, so if any man seeks to take a Christian life, the Christian should let him have it. On this view, the doctrine "resist no evil" is just an expression of contempt for earthly possessions.

But according to Augustine there are some things in this world that do have value: justice, for example, the relief of suffering, and the preservation of the Church, which Augustine equated with civilization itself. To defend these things with necessary force is not to fall prey to delusions about the good. For Augustine, then, service in the armed forces is not inconsistent with Christian values.

One difficulty for theories like Augustine's is that they seem to justify military service only when military force is used in a just cause. Unfortunately, once in the service, the man in the ranks is not in a position to evaluate the justice of his nation's cause; indeed, in many modern nations, the principle of military subordination to civilian rule prevents even generals from evaluating the purposes of war declared by political leaders. But Augustine argues that the cause of justice cannot be served without armies, and armies cannot function unless subordinates follow orders without questioning the purposes of the conflict. The necessary conditions for justice and charity require that some men put themselves in positions in which they might be required to fight for injustice.

(b) The Problem of Self-Defense

Many will agree with Augustine that most violence at the personal level—the violence of crime, vendetta, and domestic brutality, for example—goes contrary to moral principles. But most are prepared to draw the line at personal and collective self-defense. Can the obligation to be charitable justify participation in military service but stop short of justifying the use of force by private citizens, if that force is exercised to protect the weak from the oppression of the strong? Furthermore, the obligation to be charitable does not exclude acts of charity toward oneself. For Augustine, violence was a dangerous tool, best kept out of the hands of the citizens and best left strictly at the disposal of the state. Beset with fears of crime in the streets, the contemporary American is less inclined to worry about the anarchic effects of private uses of defensive force and more inclined to worry about the protection the police seem unable to provide.

For these worried people, the existence of a right to self-defense is self-evident. But the existence of this right is not self-evident to universal or private pacifists; and it was not self-evident to St. Augustine. In the Christian tradition, no right to self-defense was recognized until its existence was certified by Thomas Aquinas in the thirteenth century. Aquinas derived the right to self-defense from the universal tendency to self-preservation, assuming (contrary to Augustine) that a natural tendency must be morally right. As for the Christian duty to love one's enemy, Aquinas argued that acts of self-defense have two effects—the saving of life and the taking of life—and that self-defensive uses of force intend primarily the saving of life. This makes the use of force in self-defense a morally permissible act of charity. The right to self-defense is now generally recognized in Catholic moral theology and in Western legal systems. But it can hardly be said that Aquinas's arguments, which rely heavily on assumptions from Greek philosophy, succeed in reconciling the claims of self-defense with the prescriptions of the Sermon on the Mount.

5. ANTIWAR PACIFISM

Most people who believe in the right to personal self-defense also believe that some wars are morally justified. In fact, the notion of self-defense and the notion of just war are commonly linked; just

of people will die of allergic reactions to the vaccine. Most of the people who die from allergic reactions will be people who would not have died of the flu if the vaccination program had not been implemented. So the vaccination program will kill innocent people who would otherwise be saved if the program were abandoned. If the public health officer implements such a program, we do *not* think that he is a murderer.

Nonpacifists argue that what makes the action of Congress and the action of the public health officer morally permissible in these cases is that the deaths of the innocent, although foreseen, are not the intended goal of these policies. Congress does not want people to die on the highways; every highway death is a regrettable death. The purpose of setting the speed limit at 55 miles per hour is not to kill people but to provide a reasonable balance between safety and convenience. Likewise, it is not the purpose of the public health officer to kill people by giving them vaccine. His goal is to save lives on balance, and every death from the vaccine is a regrettable death. Likewise, in war, when civilians are killed as a result of necessary military operations, the deaths of the civilians are not the intended goal of the military operation. They are foreseen, but they are always regretted. If we do not accuse Congress of murder and the Public Health Service of murder in these cases, consistency requires that we not accuse military forces of murder when they cause civilian deaths in war, especially if every attempt is made to keep civilian deaths to a minimum.

Antiwar pacifists do not condemn the Congress and the Public Health Service in cases like these. But they assert that the case of war is different in a morally relevant way. To demonstrate the difference, antiwar pacifists provide an entirely different analysis of the moral justification for speed limits and vaccination programs. In their opinion, the facts that highway deaths and vaccination deaths are "unintended" and "regretted" is morally irrelevant. The real justification lies in the factor of consent. In the case of federal highway regulations, the rules are decided by Congress, which is elected by the people, the same people who use the highways. If Congress decides on a 55-mile-an-hour limit, this is a regulation that, in some sense, highway drivers have imposed upon themselves. Those people who die on the highway because of a higher speed limit have, in a double sense, assumed the risks generated by that speed limit: they have, through the Congress, created the risk, and by venturing onto the highway, have freely exposed themselves to the risk. The responsibility for these highway deaths, then, lies either on the drivers themselves or on the people who crashed into them—not on the Congress.

Likewise, in the case of the vaccination program, if people are warned in advance of the risks of vaccination, and if they nevertheless choose to be vaccinated, they are responsible for their own deaths should the risks be realized. According to the antiwar pacifist, it is this consent given by drivers and vaccination volunteers that justifies these policies, and it is precisely this element of consent that is absent in the case of the risks inflicted on enemy civilians in time of war.

Consider the standard textbook example of allegedly justifiable killing of civilians in time of war. Suppose that the destruction of a certain bridge is an important military objective, but if the bridge is bombed, it is very likely that civilians living close by will be killed. (The civilians cannot be warned without alerting the enemy to reinforce the bridge.) If the bridge is bombed and some civilians are killed, the bombing victims are not in the same moral category as highway victims or victims of vaccination. The bombing victims did not order the bombing of themselves through some set of elected representatives. Nor did the bombing victims freely consent to the bombing of their bridge. Nor was the bombing in any way undertaken as a calculated risk in the interest of the victims. For all these reasons, the moral conclusions regarding highway legislation and vaccination programs do not carry over to bombing of the bridge.

Nonpacifists who recognize that it will be very difficult to fight wars without bombing bridges may argue that the victims of this bombing in some sense assumed the risks of bombardment by choosing to live close to a potential military target. Indeed, it is occasionally claimed that all the civilians in a nation at war have assumed the risks of war, since they could avoid the risks of war simply by moving to a neutral country. But such arguments are strained and uncharitable, even for those rare warring nations that permit freedom of emigration. Most people consider it a major sacrifice to give up their homes, and an option that requires such a sacrifice cannot be considered an option open for free choice. The analogy between the unintended victims of vaccination and the unintended civilian victims of war seems to have broken down.

(c) The Balance of Good and Evil in War

It is left to the nonpacifist to argue that the killing of soldiers and civilians in war is in the end justifiable in order to obtain great moral goods that can be obtained only by fighting for them. Civilians have rights to life, but those rights can be outweighed by the national objectives, provided those objectives are morally acceptable and overwhelmingly important. Admittedly, this argument for killing civilians is available only to the just side in a war, but if the argument is valid, it proves that there can *be* a just side, contrary to the arguments of antiwar pacifism.

Antiwar pacifists have two lines of defense. First, they can continue to maintain that the end does not justify the means, if the means be murderous. Second, they can, and will, go on to argue that it is a tragic mistake to believe that there are great moral goods that can be obtained only by war. According to antiwar pacifists, the amount of moral good produced by war is greatly exaggerated. The Mexican War, for example, resulted in half of Mexico being transferred to American rule. This was a great good for the United States, but not a great moral good, since the United States had little claim to the ceded territory, and no great injustice would have persisted if the war had not been fought at all.

The Revolutionary War in America is widely viewed as a war that produced a great moral good; but if the war had not been fought, the history of the United States would be similar to the history of Canada (which remained loyal)—and no one feels that the Canadians have suffered or are suffering great injustices that the American colonies avoided by war. Likewise, it is difficult to establish the goods produced by World War I or the moral losses that would have ensued if the winning side, "our side," had lost. Bertrand Russell imagined the results of a British loss in World War I as follows:

> The greatest sum that foreigners could possibly exact would be the total economic rent of the land and natural resources of England. [But] the working classes, the shopkeepers, manufacturers, and merchants, the literary men and men of science—all the people that make England of any account in the world—have at most an infinitesimal and accidental share in the rental of England. The men who have a share use their rents in luxury, political corruption, taking the lives of birds, and depopulating and enslaving the rural districts. It is this life of the idle rich that would be curtailed if the Germans exacted tribute from England. (*Justice in War Time,* pp. 48–49)

But multiplying examples of wars that did little moral good will not establish the pacifist case. The pacifist must show that *no* war has done enough good to justify the killing of soldiers and the killing of civilians that occurred in the war. A single war that produces moral goods sufficient to justify its killings will refute the pacifist claim that *all* wars are morally unjustifiable. Obviously this brings the antiwar pacifist head to head with World War II.

It is commonly estimated that 35 million people died as a result of World War II. It is difficult to imagine that any cause could justify so much death, but fortunately the Allies need only justify their share of these killings. Between 1939 and 1945 Allied forces killed about 5.5 million Axis soldiers and about 1 million civilians in Axis countries. Suppose that Britain and the United States had chosen to stay out of World War II and suppose Stalin had, like Lenin, surrendered to Germany shortly after the invasion. Does avoiding the world that would have resulted from these decisions justify killing 6.5 million people?

If Hitler and Tojo had won the war, doubtless they would have killed a great many people both before and after victory, but it is quite likely that the total of *additional* victims, beyond those they killed in the war that *was* fought, would have been less than 6.5 million and, at any rate, the responsibility for those deaths would fall on Hitler and Tojo, not on Allied nations. If Hitler and Tojo had won the war, large portions of the world would have fallen under foreign domination, perhaps for a very long time. But the antiwar pacifist will point out that the main areas of Axis foreign domination—China and Russia—were not places in which the citizens enjoyed a high level of freedom *before the war began.* Perhaps the majority of people in the conquered areas would have worked out a *modus vivendi* with their new rulers, as did the majority of French citizens during the German occupation. Nor can it be argued that World War II was necessary to save six million Jews from annihilation in the Holocaust, since in fact the war did *not* save them.

The ultimate aims of Axis leaders are a matter for historical debate. Clearly the Japanese had no intention of conquering the United States, and some historians suggest that Hitler hoped to avoid war with England and America, declaring war with England reluctantly, and only after the English declared it against him. Nevertheless, popular opinion holds that Hitler intended to conquer the world, and if preventing the conquest of Russia and China could not justify six and one-half million killings, most Americans are quite confident that preventing the conquest of England and the United States does justify killing on this scale.

The antiwar pacifist disagrees. Certainly German rule of England and the United States would have been a very bad thing. At the same time, hatred of such German rule would be particularly fueled by hatred of foreigners, and hatred of foreigners, as such, is an irrational and morally unjustifiable passion. After all, if rule by foreigners were, by itself, a great moral wrong, the British, with their great colonial empire, could hardly consider themselves the morally superior side in World War II.

No one denies that a Nazi victory in World War II would have had morally frightful results. But, according to antiwar pacifism, killing six and one-half million people is also morally frightful, and preventing one moral wrong does not obviously outweigh committing the other. Very few people today share the pacifists' condemnation of World War II, but perhaps that is because the dead killed by the Allies cannot speak up and make sure that their losses are properly counted on the moral scales. Antiwar pacifists speak on behalf of the enemy dead, and on behalf of all those millions who would have lived if the war had not been fought. On this silent constituency they rest their moral case.

Review Questions

1. Characterize universal pacifists (there are two types), private pacifists, and antiwar pacifists.
2. Why doesn't Lackey accept the appeal to the Bible, or the sacredness of life, or the right to life as a good reason for accepting pacifism?
3. What is Christian pacifism and Tolstoy's argument used to defend it? Why doesn't Lackey accept Tolstoy's argument?
4. Explain Gandhi's pacifism, including *satyagraha*. What problems does Lackey raise for this view?

5. Explain Augustine's so-called limited pacifism. What problems does this view have according to Lackey?
6. State the position of antiwar pacifism. Why do antiwar pacifists believe that all wars are wrong? According to Lackey, what are the objections to antiwar pacifism, and how can antiwar pacifists reply?

Discussion Questions

1. Is Gandhi's view a defensible one? Why or why not?
2. Does the antiwar pacifist have a good reply to all the objections Lackey discusses? Are there any good objections that he does not discuss?
3. Many people think that World War II was morally justified. What does the antiwar pacifist say? What do you think?
4. According to Lackey, no great moral good was produced by the Revolutionary War in America. If America had lost this war and remained under British rule, then its history would be like that of Canada—and Canada has not suffered, he says. Do you agree? Explain your answer.

The Conduct of Just and Limited War

WILLIAM V. O'BRIEN

William V. O'Brien is professor of government at Georgetown University, Washington, D.C. He is the author of *War and/or Survival* (1969), *Nuclear War, Deterrence and Morality* (1967), *The Nuclear Dilemma and the Just War Tradition* (1986), and *Law and Morality in Israel's War with the PLO* (1991). Our reading is taken from *The Conduct of Just and Limited War* (1981).

O'Brien divides just war theory into two parts. The first, *jus ad bellum*, states conditions that should be met for a state to have the right to go to war. The second, *jus in bello*, gives principles limiting conduct in war. There are three main conditions of *jus ad bellum*: The war must be declared by a competent authority for a public purpose; there must be a just cause; and there must be a right intention that aims at peace. The condition of just cause is subdivided into four more conditions: the substance of the cause (e.g., self-defense), the form of the cause (defensive or offensive), the requirement of proportionality (the good achieved by war must be proportionate to the evil of war), and peaceful means of avoiding war must be exhausted.

Source: William V. O'Brien, *The Conduct of Just and Limited War.* Copyright © 1981 by Praeger Publishers, an imprint of Greenwood Publishing Group, Inc. Reprinted with permission of Greenwood Publishing Group, Inc., Westport, CT.

The *jus in bello* has two principles limiting conduct in war. The principle of proportion requires that the discrete military means and ends be balanced. The principle of discrimination prohibits the intentional attacks on noncombatants and nonmilitary targets.

THE ORIGINAL JUST-WAR doctrine of St. Augustine, St. Thomas, and other Scholastics emphasized the conditions for permissible recourse to war—the *jus ad bellum*. To this doctrine was added another branch of prescriptions regulating the conduct of war, the *jus in bello*. . . .

The *jus ad bellum* lays down conditions that must be met in order to have permissible recourse to armed coercion. They are conditions that should be viewed in the light of the fundamental tenet of just-war doctrine: the presumption is always against war. The taking of human life is not permitted to man unless there are exceptional justifications. Just-war doctrine provides those justifications, but they are in the nature of special pleadings to overcome the presumption against killing. The decision to invoke the exceptional rights of war must be based on the following criteria: there must be competent authority to order the war for a public purpose; there must be a just cause (it may be self-defense or the protection of rights by offensive war) and the means must be proportionate to the just cause and all peaceful alternatives must have been exhausted; and there must be right intention on the part of the just belligerent. Let us examine these criteria.

Insofar as large-scale, conventional war is concerned, the issue of competent authority is different in modern times than it was in the thirteenth century. The decentralized political system wherein public, private, and criminal violence overlapped, as well as the state of military art and science, permitted a variety of private wars. So it was important to insist that war—in which individuals would be called upon to take human lives—must be waged on the order of public authorities for public purposes. This is not a serious problem in most parts of the world today. Only states have the material capacity to wage large-scale, modern, conventional war. Two other problems do, however, exist in connection with the conditions of competent authority. First, there may be disputes as to the constitutional competence of a particular official or organ of state to initiate war. Second, civil war and revolutionary terrorism are frequently initiated by persons and organizations claiming revolutionary rights.

Most states today, even totalitarian states, have specific constitutional provisions for the declaration and termination of war. If an official or state organ violates these provisions, there may not be a valid exercise of the sovereign right to declare and wage war. In such a case the first condition of the just war might not be met. This was the charge, implicitly or explicitly, against President Johnson in the Vietnam War. Johnson never requested a declaration of war from Congress with which he shared war-making powers. War critics asserted that the undeclared war was illegal. A sufficient answer to this charge is to be found in congressional cooperation in the war effort and in the refusal of the courts to declare the war unconstitutional. . . . At this point it is sufficient to raise the issue as illustrative of the problem of competent authority within a constitutional state.

In this connection a word should be said about declaring wars. Any examination of modern wars will show that the importance of a declaration of war has diminished greatly in international practice. Because of the split-second timing of modern war, it is often undesirable to warn the enemy by way of a formal declaration. Defense measures are geared to react to hostile behavior, not declarations. When war is declared it is often an announcement confirming a condition that has already been established. Nevertheless, if a particular state's constitution does require a formal declaration of war and one is not forthcoming, the issue of competence is raised. If a public official exceeds his authority in mobilizing the people and conducting war, there is a lack of competent authority.

The second problem, however, is by far the greatest. Today, rights of revolution are frequently invoked by organizations and individuals. They clearly do not have the authority and capacity to wage war in the conventional sense. However, they do wage revolutionary war, often on an international scale. Indeed, international terrorism is one of the most pervasive and difficult problems facing the international community.

All major ideologies and blocs or alignments of states in the international system recognize the right of revolution. Usually their interpretations will emphasize the rights of revolution against others, not themselves. . . . Logically, there should be an elaborate *jus ad bellem* and *jus in bello* for revolutionary war, but development of such a doctrine has never been seriously attempted. As a result, the issues of revolutionary war tend to be treated on an ad hoc basis as special cases vaguely related to the regular categories of just war. . . .

The differences between conventional war waged by states and revolutionary war waged by rebels against states are profound. Given the formidable power of most modern governments, particularly in regard to their comparative monopoly of armed force, revolutionary rights can be asserted mainly by covert organizations waging guerrilla warfare and terrorism. The option of organizing a portion of a state and fighting a conventional civil war in the manner of the American, Spanish, or Nigerian civil wars is seldom available.

The covert, secret character of modern revolutionary movements is such that it is often hard to judge their claims to qualify as the competent authority for oppressed people. There is a decided tendency to follow the Leninist model of revolutionary leadership wherein the self-selected revolutionary elite decides on the just revolutionary cause, the means, and the circumstances of taking the initiative, all done in the name of the people and revolutionary justice. As a revolution progresses, the task of certifying competent authority continues to be difficult. Support for the revolutionary leadership is often coerced or given under conditions where there is not popular acceptance of the revolutionary authority of that leadership or its ends and means. Recognition by foreign powers of belligerency—or even of putative governmental powers—is an unreliable guide given subjective, politicized recognition policies.

To complicate matters, individuals and small groups take up revolutionary war tactics, principally terrorism in the form of airplane hijacking, hostage kidnapping, assassination, and indiscriminate bombing attacks. These acts are performed in the name of greatly varying causes, some of which could not be considered revolutionary. Sometimes the alleged justifications are political or ideological, but, on investigation, the real motivation turns out to be personal and criminal. Since most revolutionary movements manifest themselves in behavior difficult to distinguish from that of cranks and criminals, the task of sorting out revolutionaries entitled to acceptance as competent authorities is excruciating.

Two issues need to be resolved concerning revolutionary activity. First, insofar as treating revolutionaries as belligerents in a war and not as common criminals is concerned, the ultimate answer lies in the character, magnitude, and degree of success of the revolutionaries. If they can organize a government that carries on their war in a controlled fashion (assuming a magnitude requiring countermeasures that more resemble war than ordinary police operations), and if the conflict continues for an appreciable time, the revolutionaries may have won their right to be considered a competent authority for purposes of just war. Beyond this enumeration of criteria it seems unprofitable to generalize.

Second, concerning the authority of rebel leaders to mobilize the people by ordering or coercing individuals to fight for the revolutionary cause, the conscience of the individual takes precedence. Lacking any color of authority to govern, the rebels cannot of right compel participation in their cause. Needless to say, they will very probably compel participation by intimidation.

JUST CAUSE

. . . Authorities vary in their presentation of just cause, but it seems to break down into four subdivisions: the substance of the just cause, the forms of pursuing just cause, the requirement of proportionality of ends and means, and the requirement of exhaustion of peaceful remedies.

The substance of the just cause must, in Childress's formulation, be sufficiently "serious and weighty" to overcome the presumption of killing in general and war in particular. In Childress's approach, with which I am in essential agreement, this means that there must be a "competing prima facie duty or obligation" to "the prima facie obligation not to injure or kill others."[1] Childress mentions as "serious and weighty" prima facie obligations the following: (1) "to protect the innocent from unjust attack," (2) "to restore rights wrongfully denied," (3) "to reestablish a just order."

This is an adequate basis, reflective of the older just-war literature, for discussing the substance of just cause. Indeed, Childress is more explicit than many modern commentators who simply state that there should be a just cause. Still, it is only a beginning. It is unfortunate that modern moralists have generally been so concerned with the issue of putatively disproportionate means of modern war that they have neglected the prior question of the ends for which these means might have to be used (that is, just cause). In practical terms, this task of evaluating the substance of just cause leads inescapably to a comparative analysis of the characteristics of the polities or political-social systems posed in warlike confrontation. . . .

1 James F. Childress, "Just War Theories," *Theological Studies* vol. 39 (1978), pp. 428–435.

Even more difficult for those who would answer in the affirmative is the question whether the United States should intervene to protect a manifestly imperfect political-social order (South Korea, South Vietnam or, perhaps, that of a state such as Jordan, Saudi Arabia, or Pakistan). . . .

By comparison, the substantive just causes of the older just-war literature are almost insignificant. In the modern world the just cause often has to do with the survival of a way of life. Claims that this is so can be false or exaggerated, but they are often all too legitimate. They must be taken seriously in assessing the substance of just cause in modern just-war analyses.

However, passing the test of just cause is not solely a matter of positing an end that is convincingly just, although that is the indispensable starting point. It is also necessary to meet the tests posed by the other three subdivisions of just cause.

The forms of pursuing just cause are defensive and offensive wars. The justice of self-defense is generally considered to be axiomatic. Just-war doctrine, following Aristotle and St. Thomas as well as the later Scholastics, places great importance on the state as a natural institution essential for man's development. Defense of the state is prima facie of an essential social institution. So strong is the presumption in favor of the right of self-defense that the requirement of probable success, to be discussed under proportionality, is usually waived.

Offensive wars raise more complications. In classical just-war doctrine, offensive wars were permitted to protect vital rights unjustly threatened or injured. Moreover, in a form now archaic, offensive wars of vindictive justice against infidels and heretics were once permitted. Such wars disappeared with the decline of the religious, holy-war element as a cause of the rationale for wars. Thus, the forms of permissible wars today are twofold: wars of self-defense and offensive wars to enforce justice for oneself. As will be seen, even the second is now seemingly prohibited by positive international law. But in terms of basic just-war theory it remains an option. A war of vindictive justice wherein the belligerent fights against error and evil as a matter of principle and not of necessity is no longer condoned by just-war doctrine. . . .

Turning from the forms of just war we come to the heart of just cause—proportionality between the just ends and the means. This concerns the relationship between *raison d'état* (the high interests of state) and the use of the military instrument in war as the means to achieve these interests. This concept of proportionality at the level of *raison d'état* is multidimensional. To begin with, the ends held out as the just cause must be sufficiently good and important to warrant the extreme means of war, the arbitrament of arms. Beyond that, a projection of the outcome of the war is required in which the probable good expected to result from success is weighed against the probable evil that the war will cause.

The process of weighing probable good against probable evil is extremely complex. The balance sheet of good and evil must be estimated for each belligerent. Additionally, there should be a balancing of effects on individual third parties and on the international common good. International interdependence means that international conflicts are difficult to contain and that their shock waves affect third parties in a manner that must be accounted for in the calculus of probable good and evil. Moreover, the international community as such has its international common good, which is necessarily affected by any war. Manifestly, the task of performing this calculus effectively is an awesome one. But even its successful completion does not fully satisfy the demands of the just-war condition of just cause. Probing even further, the doctrine requires a responsible judgment that there is a probability of success for the just party. All of these calculations must be concluded convincingly to meet the multidimensional requirement of just cause.

Moreover, the calculus of proportionality between probable good and evil in a war is a continuing one. It should be made before the decision to go to war. It must then be reviewed

at critical points along the process of waging the war. The best informed estimates about wars are often in error. They may need revision or replacement by completely new estimates. The *jus ad bellum* requirement of proportionality, then, includes these requirements:

There must be a just cause of sufficient importance to warrant its defense by recourse to armed coercion.

The probable good to be achieved by successful recourse to armed coercion in pursuit of the just cause must outweigh the probable evil that the war will produce.

The calculation of proportionality between probable good and evil must be made with respect to all belligerents, affected neutrals, and the international community as a whole before initiating a war and periodically throughout a war to reevaluate the balance of good and evil that is actually produced by war.

These calculations must be made in the light of realistic estimates of the probability of success. . . .

There is an important qualification to the requirement of probability of success. A war of self-defense may be engaged in irrespective of the prospects for success, particularly if there is a great threat to continued existence and to fundamental values. . . .

The last component of the condition of just cause is that war be employed only as a last resort after the exhaustion of peaceful alternatives. To have legitimate recourse to war, it must be the ultima ratio, the arbitrament of arms. This requirement has taken on added significance in the League of Nations–United Nations period. It was the intention of the nations that founded these international organizations to create the machinery for peace that would replace self-help in the form of recourse to war and limit the need for collective security enforcement action to extreme cases of defiance of international law and order. There are certainly adequate institutions of international negotiations, mediation, arbitration, and adjudication to accommodate any nation willing to submit its international disputes to peaceful settlement. Indeed, the existence of this machinery for peaceful settlement has prompted international lawyers and statesmen to adopt a rough rule of thumb: the state that fails to exhaust the peaceful remedies available before resorting to war is prima facie an aggressor. . . .

RIGHT INTENTION

Among the elements of the concept of right intention, several points may be distinguished. First, right intention limits the belligerent to the pursuit of the avowed just cause. That pursuit may not be turned into an excuse to pursue other causes that might not meet the conditions of just cause. Thus, if the just cause is to defend a nation's borders and protect them from future aggressions, but the fortunes of war place the just belligerent in the position to conquer the unjust nation, such a conquest might show a lack of right intention and change the just war into an unjust war. The just cause would have been realized by a war of limited objectives rather than a war of total conquest.

Second, right intention requires that the just belligerent have always in mind as the ultimate object of the war a just and lasting peace. There is an implicit requirement to prepare for reconciliation even as one wages war. This is a hard saying. It will often go against the grain of the belligerents' disposition, but pursuit of a just and lasting peace is an essential characteristic of the difference between just and unjust war. Accordingly, any belligerent acts that unnecessarily increase the destruction and bitterness of war and thereby endanger the prospects for true peace are liable to condemnation as violations of the condition of right intention.

Third, underlying the other requirements, right intention insists that charity and love exist even among enemies. Enemies must be treated as human beings with rights. The thrust of this requirement is twofold. Externally, belligerents must act with charity toward their enemies. Internally, belligerents must suppress natural animosity and hatred, which can be sinful and injurious to the moral and psychological health of those who fail in charity. Gratuitous cruelty may be harmful to those who indulge in it as to their victims.

Right intention raises difficult moral and psychological problems. It may well be that its tenets set standards that will often be unattainable insofar as the thoughts and feelings of belligerents are concerned. War often treats individuals and nations so cruelly and unfairly that it is unrealistic to expect them to banish all hatred of those who have afflicted them. We can, however, more reasonably insist that just belligerents may not translate their strong feelings into behavior that is prohibited by the rule of right intention. A nation may feel tempted to impose a Carthaginian peace, but it may not exceed just cause by giving in to that temptation. A nation must have good reason for feeling that the enemy deserves the full force of all means available, but the requirement to build for a just and lasting peace prohibits this kind of vengeance. The enemy may have behaved abominably, engendering righteous indignation amounting to hatred, but the actions of the just belligerent must be based on charity.

Lest this appear to be so utterly idealistic as to warrant dismissal as irrelevant to the real world, let it be recalled that the greatest enemies of the modern era have often been brought around in the cyclical processes of international policies to become trusted allies against former friends who are now viewed with fear and distrust. If war is to be an instrument of policy and not, in St. Augustine's words, a "vendetta," right intention is a counsel of good policy as well as of morality. . . .

THE *JUS IN BELLO*

In the *jus in bello* that emerged rather late in the development of just-war doctrine, two basic limitations on the conduct of war were laid down. One was the principle of proportion requiring proportionality of military means to political and military ends. The other was the principle of discrimination prohibiting direct, intentional attacks on noncombatants and nonmilitary targets. These are the two categories of *jus in bello* limitations generally treated by modern workers on just war. . . .

The Principle of Proportion

In the preceding [discussion] the principle of proportion was discussed at the level of *raison d'état*. One of the criteria of just-war *jus ad bellum* requires that the good to be achieved by the realization of the war aims be proportionate to the evil resulting from the war. When the principle of proportion is again raised in the *jus in bello*, the question immediately arises as to the referent of proportionality in judging the means of war. Are the means to be judged in relation to the end of the war, the ends being formulated in the highest *raison d'état* terms? Or are intermediate political/military goals, referred to in the law-of-war literature as *raison de guerre*, the more appropriate referents in the calculus of proportionality as regards the conduct of a war?

There is no question that the ultimate justification for all means in war lies in the just cause that is a political purpose, *raison d'état*. But there are difficulties in making the ends of *raison d'état* the sole referent in the *jus in bello* calculus of proportionality. First, relation of all means to the highest ends of the war gives little rationale for or justification of discrete military means. If all means are simply lumped together as allegedly necessary for the war effort, one has to accept or reject them wholly in terms of the just cause, leaving no morality of means. The calculus of proportionality in just cause is the total good to be expected if the war is successful balanced against the total evil the war is likely to cause.

Second, it is evident that a discrete military means could, when viewed independently on the basis of its intermediary military end (*raison de guerre*), be proportionate or disproportionate to that military end for which it was used, irrespective of the ultimate end of the war at the level of *raison d'état*. If such a discrete military means were proportionate in terms of its military end, it

would be a legitimate belligerent act. If it were disproportionate to the military end, it would be immoral and legally impermissible. Thus, an act could be proportionate or disproportionate to a legitimate military end regardless of the legitimacy of the just-cause end of *raison d'état*.

Third, there is the need to be realistic and fair in evaluating individual command responsibility for belligerent acts. The need to distinguish higher political ends from intermediate military ends was acute in the war-crimes trial after World War II. It is the law of Nuremberg, generally accepted in international law, that the *raison d'état* ends of Nazi Germany were illegal aggression. But the Nuremberg and other war-crimes tribunals rejected the argument that all military actions taken by the German armed forces were war crimes per se because they were carried out in pursuance of aggressive war. The legitimacy of discrete acts of German forces was judged, inter alai, in terms of their proportionality to intermediate military goals, *raison de guerre*. This was a matter of justice to military commanders accused of war crimes. It was also a reasonable way to evaluate the substance of the allegations that war crimes had occurred.

The distinction is equally important when applied to a just belligerent. Assuming that in World War II the Allied forces were fighting a just war, it is clear that some of the means they employed may have been unjust (for example, strategic bombing of cities and the two atomic bomb attacks). It is not difficult to assimilate these controversial means into the total Allied war effort and pronounce that total effort proportionate to the just cause of the war. It is much more difficult and quite a different calculation to justify these means as proportionate to discrete military ends. Even in the absence of war-crimes proceedings, a just belligerent ought to respect the *jus in bello* standards by meeting the requirement of proportionality of means to military ends.

To be sure, it is ultimately necessary to transcend concern for the responsibility of individual military commanders and look at the objective permissibility of a military means. Thus, it may be possible and necessary to absolve a commander from responsibility for an action taken that is judged to have been disproportionate but that appeared to him to be a proportionate, reasonable military action in the light of his imperfect estimate of the situation. . . .

It would appear that analyses of the proportionality of military means will have to take a twofold form. First, any military means must be proportionate to discrete, legitimate military end. Second, military means proportionate to discrete, legitimate military ends must also be proportionate to the object of the war, the just cause. In judging the moral and legal responsibility of a military commander, emphasis should be placed on the proportionality of the means to a legitimate military end. In judging the ultimate normative permissibility, as well as the prudential advisability, of a means at the level of *raison d'état*, the calculation should emphasize proportionality to the just cause.

The focus of normative analysis with respect to a means of war will depend on the place of the means in the total pattern of belligerent interaction. Means may be divided roughly according to the traditional distinction between tactical and strategic levels of war. Tactical means will normally be judged in terms of their proportionality to tactical military ends (for example, the tactics of attacking or defending a fortified population center will normally be judged in terms of their proportionality to the military end of taking or holding the center). Strategic means will normally be judged in terms of their proportionality to the political/military goals of the war (for example, the strategy of attacking Japanese cities, first conventionally and then with atomic bombs, in order to force the surrender of Japan will be judged in terms of its proportionality to the just cause of war).

It remains clear, however, that the two levels overlap. A number of tactical decisions regarding battles for population centers may produce an overall strategic pattern that ought to enter into the highest calculation of the proportionality of a just war. The strategic decisions, on the other hand, have necessary tactical implications (for example, strategic conventional and atomic bombing of Japan was an alternative to an amphibious invasion) the conduct of which is essentially a tactical matter. The potential costs of such a tactical invasion strongly influenced the strategic choice to seek Japan's defeat by strategic bombing rather than ground conquest.

Insofar as judgment of proportionality in terms of military ends is concerned, there is a central concept appearing in all normative analyses of human behavior—the norm of reasonableness. Reasonableness must always be defined in specific context. However, sometimes patterns of behavior recur so that there are typical situations for which common models of reasonable behavior may be prescribed. In domestic law this norm is concretized through the device of the hypothetically reasonable man whose conduct sets the standard to be emulated by law-abiding persons. The reasonable commander is the counterpart of the reasonable man in the law of war. The construct of the reasonable commander is based upon the experience of military men in dealing with basic military problems.

Formulation of this experience into the kinds of working guidelines that domestic law provides, notable in the field of torts, has not advanced very far. . . . We do, however, have some instances in which this approach was followed. For example, the U.S. military tribunal in the *Hostage* case found that certain retaliatory means used in the German military in occupied Europe in World War II were reasonable in view of the threat to the belligerent occupant posed by guerrilla operations and their support by the civilian population. On the other hand, in the *Calley* case a court comprised of experienced combat officers found that Lieutenant Calley's response to the situation in My Lai was altogether unreasonable, below the standard of reasonableness expected in combat in Vietnam.[2]

2 [For a description of the My Lai Massacre, see the Problem Cases.]

The difficulty with establishing the standards of reasonableness lies in the absence of authoritative decisions that can be widely disseminated for mandatory emulation. In a domestic public order such as the United States, the legislature and the courts set standards for reasonable behavior. While the standards have supporting rationales, their greater strength lies in the fact that they are laid down by authority and must be obeyed. With the very rare exception of some of the post–World War II war-crimes cases, authoritative standards for belligerent conduct are found primarily in general conventional and customary international-law prescriptions. . . .

The Principle of Discrimination

The principle of discrimination prohibits direct intentional attacks on noncombatants and nonmilitary targets. It holds out the potential for very great, specific limitations on the conduct of just war. Accordingly, debates over the meaning of the *principle of discrimination* have become increasingly complex and important as the character of war has become more total. It is in the nature of the principle of proportion to be elastic and to offer possibilities for justifications of means that are truly necessary for efficacious military action. However, it is in the nature of the principle of discrimination to remain rigidly opposed to various categories of means irrespective of their necessity to success in war. It is not surprising, then, that most debates about the morality of modern war have focused on the principle of discrimination.

Such debates are vastly complicated by the opportunities afforded in the defiance of the principle of discrimination to expand or contract it by interpretations of its component elements. There are debates over the meaning of *direct intentional attack, noncombatants,* and *military targets.*

In order to discuss the problem of interpreting the principle of discrimination, it is necessary to understand the origins of the principle. The most fundamental aspect of the principle of discrimination lies in its direct relation to the justification for killing in war. If the presumption

against killing generally and war in particular is overcome (in the case of war by meeting the just-war conditions), the killing then permitted is limited to the enemy combatants, the aggressors. The exceptional right to take life in individual self-defense and in war is limited to the attacker in the individual case and the enemy's soldiers in the case of war. One may not attack innocent third parties as part of individual self-defense. In war the only permissible objects of direct attack are the enemy's soldiers. In both cases, the overriding moral prescription is that evil must not be done to obtain a good object. As will be seen, however, the literal application of the principle of discrimination tends to conflict with the characteristics of efficacious military action necessary to make the right of just war effective and meaningful.

However, it is important to recognize that the principle of discrimination did not find its historical origins solely or even primarily in the fundamental argument summarized above. As a matter of fact, the principle seems to have owed at least as much to codes of chivalry and to the subsequent development of positive customary laws of war. These chivalric codes and customary practices were grounded in the material characteristics of warfare during the medieval and Renaissance periods. During much of that time, the key to the conduct of war was combat between mounted knights and supporting infantry. Generally speaking, there was no military utility in attacking anyone other than the enemy knights and their armed retainers. Attacks on unarmed civilians, particularly women and children, would have been considered unchivalric, contrary to the customary law of war, and militarily gratuitous.

These multiple bases for noncombatant immunity were fortified by the growth of positive international law after the seventeenth century. In what came to be known as the Rousseau-Portalis Doctrine, war was conceived as being limited to what we could call today "counter-force warfare." Armies fought each other like athletic teams designated to represent national banners. The noncombatants were spectators to these struggles and, unless they had the bad fortune to find themselves directly on the battlefield, immune in principle from military attack. Attacks on noncombatants and nonmilitary targets were now prohibited by a rule of positive international law. Here again, the principle of discrimination was grounded in material facts, the state of the art and the limited nature of the conflicts, that continued to make possible its application. Moreover, the political philosophy of the time encouraged a separation of public armed forces and the populations they represented. All of these military and political supports for discrimination were to change with the advent of modern war.

At this point it is necessary to clarify the status of the principle of discrimination in just-war doctrine as interpreted in this chapter. It is often contended that there is an absolute principle of discrimination prohibiting any use of means that kill noncombatants. It is further contended that this absolute principle constitutes the central limitation of just war and that it is based on an immutable moral imperative that may never be broken no matter how just the cause. This is the moral axiom mentioned above, that evil may never be done in order to produce a good result. In this formulation, killing noncombatants intentionally is always an inadmissible evil.

These contentions have produced two principal reactions. The first is pacifism. Pacifists rightly argue that war inevitably involves violation of the absolute principle of discrimination. If that principle is unconditionally binding, a just war is difficult if not impossible to envisage. The second reaction to the claims of an absolute principle of discrimination is to modify the principle by some form of the principle of double effect whereby the counterforce component of a military means is held to represent the intent of the belligerent, whereas the countervalue, indiscriminate component of that means is explained as a tolerable, concomitant, unintended effect—collateral damage in contemporary strategic terms.

Paul Ramsey is unquestionably the most authoritative proponent of an absolute principle of discrimination as the cornerstone of just-war *jus*

in bello. No one has tried more courageously to reconcile this absolute principle with the exigencies of modern war and deterrence. [But] neither Ramsey nor anyone else can reconcile the principle of discrimination in an absolute sense with the strategic countervalue nuclear warfare that is threatened in contemporary deterrence. It is possible that Ramsey's version of discrimination could survive the pressures of military necessity at levels below that of strategic nuclear deterrence and war. But the fate of Ramsey's effort to reconcile an absolute moral principle of discrimination with the characteristics of modern war should indicate the grave difficulties inherent in this effort. . . .

The question then arises whether such heroic efforts to salvage an absolute principle of discrimination are necessary. As observed above, the principle of discrimination does not appear in the just-war *jus in bello* as a doctrinally established deduction from theological or philosophical first principles. Rather, it was historically the product of belligerent practice reflecting a mixture of moral and cultural values of earlier societies. Moreover, it is significant that in the considerable body of contemporary Catholic social teaching on war, embracing the pronouncements of Pope Pius XII and his successors and of Vatican II, the principle of discrimination is not prominent in any form, absolute or conditional. When weapons systems or forms of warfare are condemned, deplored, or reluctantly condoned, the rationales are so generalized that the judgments appear to be based on a mixed application of the principles of proportion and discrimination. If anything, these pronouncements seem more concerned with disproportionate rather than indiscriminate effects.

It is a curious kind of supreme, absolute principle of the just-war doctrine that slips almost imperceptibly into the evolving formulations of the authoritative texts and then is omitted as an explicit controlling rationale in contemporary judgments by the church framed in just-war terms. Moreover, the persistent reiteration by the contemporary church that legitimate self-defense is still morally permissible should imply that such defense is practically feasible; otherwise the recognition of the right is meaningless. But, as the pacifists rightly observe, self-defense or any kind of war is incompatible with an absolute principle of discrimination.

It is my contention that the moral, just-war principle of discrimination is not an absolute limitation on belligerent conduct. There is no evidence that such a principle was ever seriously advanced by the church, and it is implicitly rejected when the church acknowledges the continued right of legitimate self-defense, a right that has always been incompatible with observance of an absolute principle of discrimination. Accordingly, I do not distinguish an absolute, moral, just-war principle of discrimination from a more flexible and variable international-law principle of discrimination. To be sure, the moral, just-war understanding of discrimination must remain independent of that of international law at any given time. But discrimination is best understood and most effectively applied in light of the interpretations of the principle in the practice of belligerents. This, after all, was the principal origin of this part of the *jus in bello,* and the need to check moral just-war formulations against contemporary international-law versions is perennial.

Such a position is in no sense a retreat from a position of maximizing normative limitations on the conduct of war. In the first place, as Ramsey's brave but ultimately unsuccessful efforts have demonstrated, attachment to an absolute principle of discrimination leads either to a finding that all war is immoral and the demise of the just-war doctrine or to tortured efforts to reconcile the irreconcilable. Neither serves the purposes of the *jus in bello.* Second, the rejection of an absolute principle of discrimination does not mean an abandonment of efforts to limit war on moral grounds. The principle of discrimination remains a critical source of both moral and legal limitations of belligerent behavior. As Tucker has observed, there are significant points of limitation between the position that no injury must ever be done to noncombatants and the position that there are no restraints on countervalue warfare. The interpretations that follow here . . .

will try to balance the need to protect noncombatants with the need to recognize the legitimate military necessities of modern forms of warfare. In this process one may err one way or the other, but at least some relevant, practical guidance may be offered belligerents. Adherence to an absolute principle of discrimination usually means irrelevance to the question of limiting the means of war or unconvincing casuistry.

In search of such practical guidance one may resume the examination of the principle of discrimination as interpreted both by moralists and international lawyers. Even before the principle of discrimination was challenged by the changing realities of total war, there were practical difficulties with the definition of *direct international attack, noncombatants,* and *nonmilitary targets.* It is useful, as a starting point for analysis, to recall a standard and authoritative exposition of the principle of discrimination by Fr. Richard McCormick.

> It is a fundamental moral principle [unanimously accepted by Catholic moralists] that it is immoral directly to take innocent human life except with divine authorization. "Direct" taking of human life implies that one performs a lethal action with the intention that death should result for himself or another. Death therefore is deliberately willed as the effect of one's action. "Indirect" killing refers to an action or omission that is designed and intended solely to achieve some other purpose(s) even though death is foreseen as a concomitant effect. Death therefore is not positively willed, but is reluctantly permitted as an unavoidable by-product.[3]

As example that is frequently used in connection with this question is the use of catapults in medieval sieges of castles. The intention—indeed, the purpose—of catapulting projectiles over the castle wall was to kill enemy defenders and perhaps to break down the defenses. If noncombatants—innocents as they were called then—were killed or injured, this

---

3 "Morality of War," *New Catholic Encyclopedia* 14 (1967), p. 805.

constituted a "concomitant effect," an "undesired by-product."

The issues of intention, act, and multiple effects are often analyzed in terms of the principle of double effect, which Father McCormick's exposition employs without invoking the concept explicitly. After centuries of inconclusive efforts to apply the principle of double effect to the *jus in bello,* Michael Walzer has proposed his own version, which merits reflection and experimental application.

> The intention of the actor is good, that is, he aims narrowly at the acceptable effect; the evil effect is not one of his ends, nor is it a means to his ends, and, aware of the evil involved, he seeks to minimize it, accepting costs to himself.[4]

It is probably not possible to reconcile observance of the principle of discrimination with the exigencies of genuine military necessity without employing the principle of double effect in one form or another. However this distinction between primary, desired effect and secondary, concomitant, undesired by-product is often difficult to accept.

It is not so hard to accept the distinction in a case where the concomitant undesired effect was accidental (for example, a case where the attacker did not know that noncombatants were present in the target area). There would still remain in such a case a question as to whether the attacker ought to have known that noncombatants might be present. Nor is it so hard to accept a double-effect justification in a situation where the attacker had reason to believe that there might be noncombatants present but that this was a remote possibility. If, however, the attacker knows that there are noncombatants intermingled with combatants to the point that any attack on the military target is highly likely to kill or injure noncombatants, then the death or injury to those noncombatants is certainly "intended" or "deliberately willed," in the common usage of those words.

4 Michael Walzer, *Just and Unjust Wars* (New York: Basic Books, 1977), p. 155.

Turning to the object of the protection of the principle of discrimination—the innocents or noncombatants—another critical question of interpretation arises. How does one define noncombatants? How does one define nonmilitary targets? The assumption of separability of military forces and the populations they represented, found in medieval theory and continued by the Rousseau-Portalis Doctrine, became increasingly less valid after the wars of the French Revolution.

As nations engaged in total mobilization, one society or system against another, it was no longer possible to distinguish sharply between the military forces and the home fronts that rightly held themselves out as critical to the war effort. By the American Civil War this modern phenomenon had assumed critical importance. The material means of supporting the Confederate war effort were attacked directly and intentionally by Union forces. War in the age of the Industrial Revolution was waged against the sources of war production. Moreover, the nature of the attacks on noncombatants was psychological as well as material. Military forces have always attempted to break the will of the opposing forces as well as to destroy or scatter them. It now became the avowed purpose of military forces to break the will of the home front as well as to destroy its resources for supporting the war. This, of course, was to become a major purpose of modern strategic aerial bombardment.

To be sure, attacks on the bases of military forces have historically often been an effective strategy. But in the simpler world before the Industrial Revolution, this was not such a prominent option. When the huge conscript armies began to fight for profound ideological causes with the means provided by modern industrial mobilization and technology, the home front and consequently the noncombatants became a critical target for direct intentional attack.

The question then arose whether a civilian could be a participant in the overall was effort to such a degree as to lose his previous noncombatant immunity. Likewise, it became harder to distinguish targets that were clearly military from targets, such as factories or railroad facilities, that were of sufficient military importance to justify their direct intentional attack. It is important to note that this issue arose before the great increase in the range, areas of impact, and destructive effects of modern weaponry, conventional and nuclear. What we may term *countervalue warfare* was carried out in the American Civil War not because it was dictated by the weapons systems but because the civilian population and war-related industries and activities were considered to be critical and legitimate targets to be attacked.

In World War I this kind of attack was carried out primarily by the belligerents with their maritime blockades. Above all, these blockades caused the apparent demise of the principle of noncombatant immunity in the positive international law of war. Other factors in this demise were developments that revealed potentials not fully realized until World War II (for example, aerial bombardment of population centers and unrestricted submarine warfare). In World War II aerial bombardment of population centers was preeminent as a source of attacks on traditional noncombatants and nonmilitary targets. By this time the concept of total mobilization had advanced so far that a plausible argument could be made that vast segments of belligerent populations and complexes of industry and housing had become so integral to the war effort as to lose their noncombatant immunity.

In summary, well before the advent of weapons systems that are usually employed in ways that do not discriminate between traditional combatants and noncombatants, military and nonmilitary targets, the distinction had eroded. The wall of separation between combatants and noncombatants had been broken down by the practice of total societal mobilization in modern total war and the resulting practice of attacking directly and intentionally that mobilization base. Given these developments, it was difficult to maintain that the principle of discrimination was still a meaningful limit on war. Those who clung to the principle tended to reject modern war altogether as inherently immoral because it inherently violates the principle. In the international law of war, distinguished publicists were reduced to stating that terror bombing of noncombatants with no conceivable proximate military utility was prohibited, but that the right of noncombatants to protection otherwise were unclear. . . .

Review Questions

1. O'Brien states three conditions for permissible recourse to war. What are they?
2. What problems arise in trying to satisfy the first condition?
3. How does O'Brien explain the four subdivisions of the just cause condition?
4. What are the elements of the concept of right intention, according to O'Brien?
5. Explain the principles of proportion and discrimination as O'Brien applies them to the conduct in war.

Discussion Questions

1. O'Brien says that offensive war remains an option in just war theory. When, if ever, would an offensive war be justified?
2. According to O'Brien, right intention insists that charity and love exist even among enemies. Are charity and love compatible with killing and injuring people?
3. O'Brien thinks that the bombing of Hiroshima and Nagasaki was allowed by just war theory. Do you agree? Didn't this killing of 200,000 innocent people violate the principle of discrimination?

The Morality of Terrorism

HAIG KHATCHADOURIAN

Haig Khatchadourian is emeritus professor of philosophy at the University of Wisconsin, Milwaukee. He is the author of nine books (one of them a book of poetry), including *A Critical Study in Method* (1971), *The Concept of Art* (1971), *Philosophy of Language and Logical Theory* (1995) *Community and Communitarianism* (1999), and *War, Terrorism, Genocide, and the Quest for Peace* (2003). Our reading is taken from *The Morality of Terrorism*.

Khatchadourian begins with the problem of defining terrorism. He argues that the definitions of Lackey and others are inadequate because they are too broad, or too narrow, or beg ethical issues. Instead of giving a formal definition, he says that the core meaning of terrorism includes the notion that terrorist acts are acts of coercion or force aiming at monetary gain, revenge, a political end, or a moral/religious end. So there are four types of terrorism: predatory, retaliatory, political, and moral/religious terrorism. He adds that the "bifocal character" of terrorism, the fact that it aims at both immediate victims and "the victimized," is what distinguishes terrorism from other uses of coercion or force.

Then Khatchadourian turns to the morality of terrorism. He argues that terrorism in all its forms is always wrong. It flagrantly violates three principles of just war theory: the principles of necessity, proportion, and discrimination. (The principle of proportion has two different forms, a political form applying to the right to go to war and a military form applying to the conduct of war.) In addition, all but the moralistic/religious type of terrorism violate the condition of a just cause. Finally, Khatchadourian argues that terrorism violates human rights, including the basic right to be treated as a moral person.

TERRORISM: WHAT'S IN A NAME?

WHAT TERRORISM IS or how the word should be employed is a much vexed question, and many definitions of it have been proposed. Some of the conceptual reasons for the lack of agreement on its meaning will become clearer as I proceed, but the fact that the term is almost invariably used in an evaluative—indeed, highly polemical and emotionally charged—way makes the framing of a neutral definition a difficult task. It is probably no exaggeration to say that, at present, it is as emotional a word as "war." In fact, some think of terrorism as a kind of war, and the mere mention of the word arouses similar anxieties and fears. This was particularly true at the time this was being written, against the backdrop of the Gulf War and President Saddam Hussein's repeated warnings of terrorism against American and European interests world-wide. Not surprisingly, therefore, terrorism is very widely condemned as a major evil plaguing the last decades of the Twentieth century, a century already drenched with the blood of the innocent and the noninnocent is a long series of wars, revolutions, civil wars, and other forms of violence.

Source: From Haig Khatchadourian, *The Morality of Terrorism* (New York: Peter Lang, 1998), pp. 1–38. Footnotes renumbered. Used by permission of the publisher.

The widespread condemnation of terrorism as an unmitigated evil stems in part from the fact that some of those governments or countries, political systems, or regimes, that are the main targets, particularly of state or state-sponsored political violence, use the word as a political-psychological weapon in their fight against the perpetrators and their avowed causes—for example, national liberation from foreign occupation or the overthrow of an oppressive indigenous system or regime. In fighting terrorism targeted at them, the victim groups or countries tend to indiscriminately label all their enemies as "terrorists," including those who practice the least violent kinds of protest, thus stretching the word's already loose usage and vague meaning beyond reason.[1] Despite its notorious vagueness and looseness, some overlap among the multiplicity of the word's definitions and characterizations exists. Quite a number of definitions in the literature, as well as characterizations in the media and in everyday discourse, include the idea that terrorism is the threat or the actual use of violence—the unlawful use of force[2]—directed against civilians (e.g. noncombatants in wartime) *and they alone,* sometimes with the addition of the words, *"for political* purposes." In that respect the moral philosopher Douglas Lackey's definition is typical. With wartime terrorism in mind, he writes: "What separates the terrorist from the traditional revolutionary is a persistent refusal to direct violence at military objectives. Terrorism, on this account, is the threat or use of violence against noncombatants for political purposes. In ordinary war, the deaths of civilians are side effects of military operations directed against military targets. In terrorist operations, the civilian is

the direct and intentional target of attack."[3] The same putative core of meaning occurs in other definitions I shall consider.

Although I shall argue that this and similar definitions of "terrorism" are inadequate, Lackey is right in rejecting the definition of former Vice-President George Bush's Task Force on Combating Terrorism, according to which terrorism is "the unlawful use or threat of violence against persons or property to further political or social objectives."[4] That definition, Lackey notes, is too broad, but his own definition suffers from the opposite defect, although it has the merit of not confining the victims of terrorism to civilians. Another example of a too-broad definition is the Task Force's "the threatened or actual use of force or violence to attain a political goal through fear, coercion, or intimidation."[5]

The preceding and most of the other definitions that have been proposed share a more fundamental defect, one that will be noted as we proceed.

Other proposed definitions I have examined[6] are also either too broad or too narrow, or both—a problem faced by "essentialist" definitions in general—often in addition to other defects. Some definitions are too restrictive, being limited to one form of terrorism, for example, political terrorism in the usual, restricted meaning

---

1 A notorious example, which carries this tendency to absurdity, is the late Mr. Rabin's calling the "stone children" of the Palestinian intifada "terrorists" in front of American television cameras. Mr. Rabin himself was murdered by a Jewish terrorist.

2 This is false in terrorism practiced by a ruling dictator or military junta, whenever the government's (or its military's) terrorist activities conform to (unjust) laws decreed by the dictator or junta.

3 Douglas Lackey, *The Ethics of War and Peace* (Englewood Cliffs, NJ, 1989), 85.

4 "Report of Vice-President's Task Force on Combating Terrorism," in Lackey, *Ethics,* 85.

5 Charles A. Russell et al., "Out-Inventing the Terrorist," in *Terrorism, Theory and Practice,* Yonah Alexander et al., eds. (Boulder, CO, 1979), 4. In note 2, p. 37, the authors add: "'Political' is understood in this usage to connote the entire range of social, economic, religious, ethnic, and governmental factors impacting on a body politic, stressing the notions of power and influence. The ideal definition is one that both the adherents and abhorrers of terrorism could agree upon."

6 According to Leonard B. Weinberg and Paul Davis, *Introduction to Political Terrorism* (New York, 1989), 3, more than one hundred separate definitions have been proposed by different analysts over the years. See also Harold J. Vetter et al., *Perspectives on Terrorism* (Pacific Grove, CA, 1990), 3, where it is stated that the definitions were formulated between 1936 and 1983.

of the word.[7] Still other definitions or characterizations fail because they are overtly or covertly normative (condemnatory) rather than, as definitions ought to be, neutral or nonevaluative. Former President Ronald Reagan's statement that terrorism is the deliberate maiming or killing of innocent people, and his characterization of terrorists as "base criminals," clearly beg the ethical issues.[8] A fuller definition that suffers from the same flaw among others, is proposed by Burton Leiser. Part of his definition is:[9]

> *Terrorism* is any organized set of acts of violence designed to destroy the structure of authority which normally stands for security, or to reinforce and perpetuate a governmental regime whose popular support is shaky. It is a policy of seemingly senseless, irrational, and arbitrary murder, assassination, sabotage, subversion, robbery and other forms of violence, all committed with dedicated indifference to existing legal and moral codes or with claims to special exemption from conventional social norms.

ELEMENTS OF TERRORISM

The main forms of terrorism in existence in the present-day world share at least five important aspects or elements which an adequate description of terrorism must include. They are:

1. The historical and cultural, including the socioeconomic root causes of its prevalence (e.g., the lack or loss of a homeland).

2. The immediate, intermediate and long-range or ultimate goals. Retaliation is an example of the first, while publicity is an example of the second. The regaining of a lost homeland, the acquisition or exercise of power [by a state], . . . or enforcement

of [its] authority,"[10] (which F. J. Hacker calls terrorism from above[11]), or the challenge to . . . [a state's] authority (which he calls terrorism from below) are examples of long range terrorist goals.

3. The third aspect or element consists in the forms and methods of coercion and force[12] generally resorted to to terrorize the immediate victims and to coerce[13] those who are seriously affected by the terrorism, the victimized. The latter are the individuals, groups, governments, or countries that are intimately connected with the immediate targets and who are themselves the real albeit indirect targets of the terrorist acts.[14] The forms and methods of coercion and force resorted to define the different *species* or *forms* of terrorism of any given *type*.

4. The nature or kinds of organizations and institutions, or the political systems, practicing or sponsoring the terrorism. For example, in state terrorism the terrorism is practiced by agents of a state, while in state-sponsored terrorism the terrorism is financially, militarily, or in other ways supported but not directly conducted by the sponsoring state or states.

5. The social, political, economic or military context or circumstances in which the terrorism occurs is also important and must be considered. For example, whether the

---

7 For example, Weinberg and Davis' definition in their *Introduction*, 3ff.

8 Quoted in Haig Khatchadourian, "Terrorism and Morality," *Journal of Applied Philosophy*, 5, no. 2 (October 1988): 131.

9 Burton M. Leiser, *Liberty, Justice, and Morals* (New York, 1979), 375. Italics in original.

10 Vetter et al., *Perspectives*, 8.

11 Frederick J. Hacker, *Crusaders, Criminals, Crazies* (New York, 1977), quoted in Vetter et al., 8.

12 I use "force" because it is morally neutral or near-neutral, unlike the more common "violence."

13 Weinberg and Davis, Introduction, 6, state: "The objective purpose of harming immediate victims is subordinate to the purpose of sending a message to some broader target population [the 'victimized']." Although this statement shows their recognition of the bifocal character of terrorism, the idea of "sending a message" is too general and vague to be of much service.

14 I borrow "immediate victim" from Abraham Edel, "Notes on Terrorism," in *Values in Conflict*, Burton M. Leiser, ed. (New York, 1981), 458.

terrorism occurs in time of peace or in wartime.[15] In the latter case, there is also an important ethical dimension in relation to terrorist violence or threats to noncombatants, just as in the case of precision "saturation" bombing of towns and cities in Twentieth century warfare. This would become incalculably more important in the case of possible nuclear terrorism.[16]

The one form of terrorism to which (1) above does not normally apply is predatory terrorism—terrorism motivated by greed. But predatory terrorism is relatively unimportant, especially for a discussion of the morality of terrorism such as the present one, since it is clearly immoral. Although seriously flawed, Leiser's definition noted earlier has the merit of incorporating several of the aspects of terrorism I have mentioned. But it fails to spell out the various sorts of causes of terrorism and makes only a passing mention of what it calls the terrorists' "political ends."[17]

DEFINING "TERRORISM"

A fully adequate characterization or formal definition of "terrorism" must be as neutral as possible and not beg the issue of the morality of terrorism in general, in addition to reflecting the five aspects or dimensions of terrorism distinguished above—notwithstanding the word's almost invariably negative connotations, particularly in the Western world. . . .

In the current literature the question of whether noninnocents can be included among the immediate victims of terrorism appears to be a very unsettled question. The absence of clarity and fixity—indeed, the ambivalence and uncertainty in current employments of the word—reflect the different users' stand on the *morality* of terrorism and the

morality, especially, of the unlawful use of force in general. These uncertainties are intimately connected with uncertainties concerning the distinction between terrorism and "freedom fighting," such as a rebellion, a civil war, an uprising, or a guerrilla war aiming, for example, at national liberation. Those who consider the harming of innocent persons an essential feature of terrorism would tend to consider "freedom fighting" as involving, *inter alia,* the maiming, killing or coercing of *non*innocents. That would allow "political assassination" to be classified as a species of "freedom fighting." Leiser states that guerrilla warfare is characterized by small-scale, unconventional, limited actions carried out by irregular forces "*against regular military forces, their supply lines, and communications.*"[18] That description would be perfectly in order provided we stipulate that the targeted soldiers are in the army of their own free will.

The preceding discussion indicates that in addition to being open textured and vague, the various current evaluative concepts of terrorism, like all other evaluative concepts, are, in W. B. Gallie's phrase, "essentially contested."[19] Yet like most vague and unsettled expressions "terrorism" has a "common core of meaning" in its different usages. This core of meaning includes the notion that terrorist acts are acts of coercion or of actual use of force,[20] aiming at monetary gain (*predatory terrorism*), revenge (*retaliatory terrorism*), a political end (*political terrorism*), or a putative moral/religious end (*moralistic/religious terrorism*).[21]

---

18 Ibid., 381. Italics in original.

19 W. B. Gallie, "Essentially Contested Concepts," *Proceedings of the Aristotelian Society,* n.s., 56 (March 1956), 180ff. But Gallie maintains that a concept must have certain characteristics in addition to appraisiveness (he enumerates them on pp. 171–172) to be "essentially contested" in his sense.

20 Those who use "terrorism" as a condemnatory term would substitute "violence" for "force."

21 I borrow the categories "predatory" and "moralistic" from Edel, "Notes on Terrorism," 453. Some but not all moralistic terrorism is political terrorism, or vice versa. "Narcoterrorism" is a special subform of predatory terrorism, not a separate, additional form of terrorism. For this fundamental distinction at the heart of terrorism as a kind of use of force or violence for certain ends, I am indebted to Edel's essay.

---

15 This and the next section are largely reproduced, with some stylistic and substantive changes, from my "Terrorism and Morality."

16 Cf. Joel Kovel, *Against The State Of Nuclear Terror* (Boston, MA, 1983), Robert J. Lifton and Richard Falk, *Indefensible Weapons* (New York, 1982), and Helen Caldicott, *Missile Envy, The Arms Race and Nuclear War* (New York, 1986).

17 Leiser, *Liberty, Justice and Morals,* 375.

What is absolutely essential for an adequate concept of terrorism and helps distinguish it from all other uses of force or coercion, but which most definitions I have come across lack, is what I shall call terrorism's "bifocal" character. I mean the crucial distinction between (a) the "immediate victims," the individuals who are the immediate targets of terrorism, and (b) "the victimized," those who are the indirect but real targets of the terrorist acts. Normally the latter are individual governments or countries or certain groups of governments or countries, or specific institutions or groups within a given country. The ultimate targets may also be certain social, economic or political systems or regimes which the terrorists dislike and hope to change or destroy by their terrorist activities. . . .

THE MORALITY OF TERRORISM AND A JUST WAR THEORY

Although the literature on terrorism is constantly growing, very little has been written about the morality of terrorism; perhaps because the writers take it for granted that terrorism is a scourge, always morally reprehensible and wrong: note for instance the common equation of terrorism with murder. . . .

This is not a very auspicious beginning for a moral evaluation of terrorism. From the fact that terrorist acts, including the killing of immediate victims, are prohibited in many if not all municipal legal systems, it does not follow that some or all such acts are *morally* wrong. Calling terrorist killings "murder" begs the complex ethical issues involved. . . .

Whether . . . some terrorists acts . . . are morally justified is an important question and will be discussed in relation to just war theory. . . .

The traditional conditions of a just war are of two sorts: conditions of justified going to war (*jus ad belum*) and conditions of the just prosecution of a war in progress (*jus in bello*). One of the fundamental conditions of the latter kind is that

> The destruction of life and property, even enemy life and property, is inherently bad. It follows that military forces should cause no more

destruction than is strictly necessary to achieve their objectives. (Notice that the principle does not say that whatever is necessary is permissible, but that everything permissible must be necessary). This is the principle of necessity: that *wanton* destruction is forbidden. More precisely, the principle of necessity specifies that a military operation is forbidden if there is some alternative operation that causes less destruction but has the same probability of producing a successful military result.[22]

Another fundamental condition is the principle of discrimination or noncombatant immunity, which prohibits the deliberate harming—above all the killing—of innocent persons. In "Just War Theory" William O'Brien defines that condition as the principle that "prohibits direct intentional attacks on noncombatants and nonmilitary targets,"[23] and Douglas Lackey, in *The Ethics of War and Peace,* characterize it as "the idea that . . . civilian life and property should not be subjected to military force: military force must be directed only at military objectives."[24] A third fundamental condition is the principle of proportion, as "applied to discrete military ends."[25] That condition is defined by O'Brien as "requiring proportionality of means to political and military ends."[26] Or as Lackey states it, it is the idea that "the amount of destruction permitted in pursuit of a military objective must be proportionate to the importance of the objective. This is the *military* principle of proportionality (which must be distinguished from the *political* principle of proportionality in the *jus ad bellum*)."[27]

My contention is that these three principles, duly modified or adapted, are analogically applicable to all the types of terrorism, and that

22 Douglas P. Lackey, *The Ethics of War and Peace* (Englewood Cliffs, NJ, 1989), 59. Italics in original.

23 William O'Brien, "Just-War Theory," in Burton M. Leiser *Liberty, Justice, and Morals,* 2nd ed. (New York, 1979), 39. This section is in large measure reproduced from sections III–V of Haig Khatchadourian, "Terrorism and Morality," *Journal of Applied Philosophy,* 5, no. 2 (1958): 134–143.

24 Lackey, *Ethics,* 59.

25 Ibid., 37.

26 Ibid., 30.

27 Ibid., 59. Italics in original.

they are flagrantly violated by them. Indeed, all but the moralistic/religious type of terrorism violate a further condition of just war theory. I refer to the first and most important condition of *jus ad bellum* and one of the most important conditions of a just war in general: the condition of just cause. . . .

Of the four main types of terrorism, predatory, retaliatory and nonmoralistic/religious terrorism clearly run afoul of the just cause condition, understood—in a nutshell—as the self-defensive use of force. Conceivably only some acts of moralistic and moralistic-political/religious terrorism can satisfy that condition. It is clear that the former three types of terrorism violate that condition.

Let us begin with predatory terrorism, terrorism motivated by greed. Like "ordinary" acts of armed robbery, of which it is the terrorist counterpart, predatory terrorism is a crime and is morally wrong. Both cause terror and indiscriminately hurt whoever happens to be where they strike. Indeed, hostage-taking by armed robbers in hopes of escaping unscathed by forcing the authorities to give them a getaway car or plane is an additional similarity to terrorism. It can even be regarded as predatory terrorism itself, particularly if it is systematic and not a onetime affair, since both political and moralistic terrorism tend to be systematic. . . . Even then, armed robbery involving hostage-talking, must be distinguished from the kind of armed robbery that political or moralistic terrorists may indulge in to raise money for their particular political/moralistic/religious ends.

Nonetheless, bona fide predatory (and even retaliatory) terrorism is often unsystematic; like ordinary armed robbery, it may also be a one-time thing. Some well-known terrorist airplane hijackings in the United States for monetary gain have been one-time incidents, although in all but one instance I know of, that was simply because the hijackers were apprehended!

Like predatory terrorism, retaliatory terrorism may or may not be systematic. International terrorism usually includes a systematic policy of retaliation against a hated, enemy state or its citizens. A notorious example a few years ago was the retaliatory terrorism against the United States and its interests, sponsored by Libya, Syria, and/or Iran.

More important for the present discussion, retaliatory terrorism violates, among other moral rules, the just cause condition and the principles of justice, and is consequently wrong. For what is retaliation but another (more euphemistic?) word for revenge, which is incompatible with self-defense as well as due process. That is no less true in war, if retaliatory terrorism is practiced by a country in its efforts to defend itself against aggression. For example, if an attempt is made on the life of the aggressor country's head of state by agents of the victim state in retaliation for attacks on its territory, the assassination attempt would be (a) an act of *terrorism* if it is *intended* to pressure the aggressor's military to end the aggression. But despite its *goal* and the victim's perception of it as part of its national self-defense, it remains (b) an act of retaliation, not an act of self-defense.

What I have said about predatory and retaliatory terrorism in relation to just cause applies to nonmoralistic political terrorism, to terrorism whose political goals are *not* moral. An example is when a revolutionary group commits acts of terrorism against a legitimate, democratically elected government it wants to overthrow out of lust for power.

By definition, moralistic terrorism satisfies just cause if "just cause" is interpreted broadly to mean a morally justifiable cause, for example, political terrorism strictly as part of a national liberation movement against a foreign occupier or indigenous oppressive regime. It *may* also satisfy the condition of right intention. Consequently, I shall turn to the other two conditions of just war I mentioned earlier, to ascertain whether even such terrorism can be morally justifiable.

Principle of Necessity and Terrorism

The principle of necessity states that "*wanton destruction* [in war] is forbidden. More precisely, the principle . . . specifies that a military operation is forbidden if there is some alternative operation that causes less destruction but has the same probability of producing a successful military result."[28] *Pace* Lackey, who regards it as a more precise form of the condition, it is distinct from, although closely related to, the principle that wanton destruction is forbidden in war. If a war *is* a last resort, it would follow that the destruction of life and property is necessary, not wanton. And if it is necessary, it *is* a last resort.

It is clear that predatory terrorism is always a wanton destruction of life or property, and the same is true of retaliatory terrorism; however, the concept of "last resort" is inapplicable to them. If Iran had chosen to sue the United States for compensation or reparation at the International Court of Justice at the Hague, for the shooting down an Iranian airbus during the Iraq-Iran war, that would have constituted a peaceful, nonviolent *alternative* to any terrorist retaliation against the United States Iran may have sponsored in its aftermath, such as the destruction of Pan Am Flight 103 over Lockerbie, Scotland, which some believe was instigated and financed by Iran and implemented by a notorious Palestinian terrorist. (The United States has steadfastly held Libya, and possibly Syria, responsible for that atrocity.) Logically, retaliation on the one hand and reparation, compensation, or restitution, or other peaceful ways of undoing or rectifying a wrong, are horses of very different colors.

Principle of Discrimination and Terrorism

In many acts of terrorism some or all of the immediate victims and/or victimized are innocent persons, in no way morally connected with or in any degree responsible for the wrong moralistic terrorism is intended to help rectify, hence for the physical or mental harm that the terrorists inflict on them. In predatory terrorism the immediate victims and the victimized are, almost without exception, innocent persons. That is also often true of retaliatory terrorism, at least as far as the immediate victims are concerned. Two very tragic examples in recent memory are the hijacking of the *Achille Lauro,* and the destruction of the Pan Am plane over Lockerbie. In political and political-moralistic terrorism, whether in wartime or in time of peace, some of the immediate victims or some of the victimized are likely to be innocent persons; but some may be noninnocents, such as members (especially high-ranking members) of the military, who are morally responsible for the real or imagined wrong that triggers the terrorism.

The problem of distinguishing innocent and noninnocent persons in relation to different types and forms of terrorism, except terrorism in war, is on the whole less difficult that the much-vexed corresponding problem in relation to war. My position, *mutatis mutandis* in relation to war, simply stated, is this: (1) "Innocence" and "noninnocence" refer to *moral* innocence and noninnocence, relative to the particular acts, types, or forms of terrorism T. (2) Innocence and non-innocence are a matter of degree. (3) A perfectly innocent person is one who has no moral responsibility, *a fortiori,* no causal responsibility at all, for any wrong that gave rise to T. A paradigmatically noninnocent person is someone who has an appreciable degree of moral, hence direct or indirect causal responsibility for the wrong, triggering T.[29] Between that extreme and paradigmatic noninnocents there would be, theoretically, cases of decreasing moral responsibility corresponding to decreasing degrees of causal responsibility. Here the targets would be noninnocent in some but lesser degree than in paradigmatic cases of noninnocence. (4) Moral responsibility may be direct or indirect, by virtue of a person's direct or indirect role in T's causation—where T is triggered or has its root cause(s) in some real injustice or wrong. The degree of a person's innocence may therefore

---

28 Lackey, *Ethics,* 59. Italics in original.

29 What constitutes an "appreciable degree" of moral responsibility would of course be a matter of controversy.

also vary in that way. Everyone whose actions are a proximate cause of the wrong is noninnocent in a higher degree than those whose responsibility for it is indirect. In particular cases it is always possible in principle to ascertain whether an individual is, causally, directly involved. Generally it is also actually possible, although often quite difficult, to do so in practice. Ascertaining who is indirectly responsible and who is not at all responsible is another matter. Since we are mainly concerned with the theoretical problem of the morality of terrorism, that is not too disquieting. But it is of the essence from the point of view of would-be terrorists and that of the law—unless the terrorists happen to be deranged and target innocent individuals or groups they imagine to be morally responsible for the grievances they are out to avenge or redress. Further, the very life of some individuals may depend on the potential terrorists' ability to distinguish innocent from noninnocent persons or groups. Political, retaliatory, or moralistic terrorists, driven by passion or paranoia, often baselessly enlarge, sometimes to a tragically absurd extent, the circle of alleged noninnocent persons. They sometimes target individuals, groups or whole nations having only a tenuous relation, often of a completely innocent kind, to those who have wronged their compatriots or ancestors, stolen their land, and so on. The example given earlier of terrorists striking at the high-ranking officials of governments whose predecessors committed crimes against their people, illustrates this. Another example is terrorism targeting innocent persons presumed to be guilty by association, simply because they happen to be of the same race, nationality, or religion, or enjoy the same ethnic heritage as those deemed responsible for the hurt.

An extreme, horrifying kind of justification of the targeting of completely innocent persons was brought to my attention by Anthony O'Heare.[30] It involves the justification one sometimes hears of the killing of holidaymakers, travelers, and others, in Israel and other terrorists targets,

"on the ground that . . . the very fact that they were contributing to the economy and morale of the targeted country [unwittingly] implicated them." As O'Heare comments, that defense is "a disgusting piece of casuistry." Its implications, I might add, are so far-reaching as to be positively frightening. If the travelers or holidaymakers were guilty of a crime against, say, the Palestinian people, as is claimed, then by parity of reasoning all individuals, institutions, groups or peoples, all countries or nations that have any kind of economic dealings with Israel and so contribute to its economy would likewise be guilty of a crime against the Palestinian people and so may be justifiably targeted! But then why exempt those *Arabs* who live in Israel and even those *Palestinians* residing in the West Bank or in the Gaza Strip who are employed in Israel—indeed, all those who spend any amount of money there—from guilt?

Finally, to be able to protect individuals against terrorism, law enforcement agencies as well as governments in general need to be able to protect individuals against terrorism, need to make reliable predictions about who is a likely target of known terrorist organizations. Yet in few other kinds of coercison or other uses of force is the element of unpredictability and surprise greater or the strikes more impelled by emotion and passion than in terrorism. This problem will be later taken up again in a discussion of responses to terrorism.

Principles of Proportion and Terrorism

In addition to its violation of the moral principles considered above, terrorism may appear to violate two other principles of just war theory: (1) the *political* principle of proportion of *jus ad bellum* and (2) the *military* principle of proportion of *jus in bello*. The former is stated by William O'Brien as requiring that "the good to be achieved by the realisation of the war aims be proportionate to the evil resulting from the war."[31] And "the calculus of proportionality in

---

30 Private communication to the author.

31 O'Brien, "Just-War Theory," 37.

just cause [that is, the political purpose, *raison d'etat,* "the high interests of the state"] is to the total good to be expected if the war is successful balanced against the evil the war is likely to cause."[32] Lackey describes the political principle of proportionality as stipulating that "a war cannot be just unless the evil that can reasonably be expected to ensue from the war is less than the evil that can reasonably be expected to ensue if the war is not fought."[33]

The military counterpart of the political principle is described by Lackey as the idea that "the amount of destruction permitted in pursuit of a military objective must be proportionate to the importance of the objective. It follows from the military principle of proportionality that certain objectives should be ruled out of consideration on the ground that too much destruction would be caused in obtaining them."[34]

As in the case of war, the main problem facing any attempt to apply the *political* principle of proportion to terrorism is the difficulty of reaching even the roughest estimate of the total expected good *vis-a-vis* the total evil likely to be caused by a series of connected acts of political or *moralistic/religious* terrorism. The crudest estimates of the expected good of some political-moralistic/religious cause against the suffering or death of even one victim or victimized person are exceedingly difficult to come by. And if we turn from isolated acts of political-moralistic/religious terrorism to a whole series of such acts extending over a period of years or decades, as with Arab or IRA terrorism, the task becomes utterly hopeless. For how can we possibly measure the expected good resulting from the creation of, for example, an independent Catholic Northern Ireland or a Catholic Northern Ireland united with the Irish Republic, and compare it with the overall evil likely to be the lot of the Ulster Protestants in such an eventuality or on different scenarios of their eventual

fate—then add the latter evil to the evils consisting in and consequent upon all the acts of terrorism that are supposed to help realise the desired good end? I see no possible way in which these factors can be quantified, hence added or subtracted.[35]

It seems then that we cannot ascertain whether political or moralistic/religious terrorism sometimes or always violates the political principle of proportion. However, it is a patent fact that no political or moralistic/religious terrorist movement in this century—whether Palestinian, Lebanese, Libyan, Syrian, Iranian, Irish, or Algerian—has succeeded in realizing its ultimate or overall political or moralistic objectives. Moreover, these movements have no more chance of success in the future than they have had so far. Palestinian terrorism is typical. Since, in Israel and the West, terrorism is almost synonymous with murder, it is not surprising that instead of helping the eminently just Palestinian cause, Palestinian acts of terrorism (as distinguished from Palestinian resistance, e.g. the intifada) from the very start have hurt the cause almost beyond repair. Not only has terrorism failed to win the Palestinians their human and other rights or brought them any closer to selfdetermination: it has created strong public sympathy in the West for Israel and turned public attitudes strongly against the Palestinians, or at least their leadership, and has further increased Israeli security concerns.[36] This does enable us, I think, to conclude after all that the preceding types of terrorism are indeed in serious violation of the political principle of proportion. For the result of tallying the evils of terrorist acts in human pain

32 Ibid.
33 Lackey, *Ethics,* 40.
34 Ibid., 59.

35 For the special significance of this in relation to revolutionary terrorism, see Chapter 4.
36 A personal note: My own moral condemnation of terrorism and my conviction that it was bound to hurt rather than help the Palestinian cause led me, soon after the first Palestinian skyjacking, to send an open letter to the PLO leadership. In this letter I pointed these things out and pleaded that the PLO put an end to such acts. For rather obvious reasons the Beirut publication to which I sent the letter could not publish it.

and suffering, death and destruction, against the nonexistent overall benefits leaves a huge surplus of unmitigated evil on the negative side. I refer not only to the evil inflicted by the terrorists upon their victims and the victimized but also the evil they draw upon themselves and their families by risking loss of life, limb, or liberty in ultimately futile pursuit of their dangerous and violent objectives.

We now turn to the military principle of proportionality—in O'Brien's words, the principle that "a discrete military means . . . when viewed independently on the basis of its intermediate military end (*raison de guerre*), must . . . be proportionate . . . to that military end for which it was used, irrespective of the ultimate end of the war at the level of *raison d'etat*."[37] This principle, applied to discrete military means, O'Brien observes, is in line with the law of Nuremberg, which judged the "legitimacy of discrete acts of the German forces, . . . inter alia, in terms of their proportionality to intermediate military goals, *raison de guerre*. . . . It was a reasonable way to evaluate the substance of the allegations that war crimes had occurred."[38]

The present form of the principle *can* be applied, *mutatis mutandis,* to discrete acts of terrorism provided that their probable intermediate results can be roughly assessed. For example, in evaluating the morality of the *Achille Lauro* seajacking, the short-term and intermediate "political" gains the terrorists expected to receive must be weighed, if possible, against the killing of an innocent passenger and the terrorism visited on the other passengers on board. It can be safely said that apart from the damage the seajacking did to the PLO and to the Middle East peace process as a whole, whatever benefit the seajackers expected to reap from their acts,[39] such as publicity and the dramatization of the plight of the Palestinians under Israeli military rule in the occupied territories, was vastly outweighed by the evils the seajacking resulted in.[40] More important still, the actual and not (as in O'Brien's formulation of the principle) merely the expected outcome of acts of terrorism, good and bad, must be weighed, if possible, against each other. That is, actual proportionality must obtain if, in retrospect, the acts are to be objectively evaluated. But to do so is precisely to assess the outcomes of the acts in terms of consequentialist criteria, and so will be left for later consideration.

The same general factors need to be weighed for the evaluation of other discrete acts of terrorism in relation to the military principle of proportionality; for example, the assassination of members of the Israeli Olympic team in Munich in 1972, the hijacking of TWA flight 847 in Athens, Greece, in 1985, the downing of Pan Am flight 103 over Lockerbie, Scotland, in 1989, and so on.

Terrorism and Human Rights

It can be safely said that the belief that all human beings have a (an equal) human right to life, at least in the minimal sense of a negative right to life—a right not to be unjustly or wrongly killed—is held by anyone who believes in the existence of human rights at all. That idea is also found in the United Nations *Universal Declaration of Human Rights*. Thus, Article 3 states, among other things, that "Everyone has the right to life." The importance of our acknowledging such a universal human right is evident: the protection of human life is the sine qua non of the individual's capacity to realize anything and everything—any and all values—a

37 O'Brien, "Just-War Theory," 37.
38 Ibid., 38.
39 One of the seajackers stated after being captured that the original objective was a suicide mission in Israel. That objective, of course, was not realized.

40 Note that the question whether the capture, trial, and almost certain punishment of the seajackers and others implicated in the act is to be judged a good or an evil to be added to one or the other side of the balance sheet, partly depends for its answer on the evaluation of the act itself as morally justified or unjustified. I say "partly depends" because the legal implications of the act are also relevant.

human being is capable of realizing in relation to himself or herself and others. But even if one does not acknowledge a distinct human right, a right to life as such, I believe that one is forced to acknowledge the existence of some protective norms, such as other human rights and/or principles of fairness and justice, that prohibit, except in very special circumstances, the taking of human life. For instance, justice prohibits the execution of an innocent person for a crime he or she has not committed. Or the moral protection of human life can be placed under the protective umbrella of, for example, a human right to be treated as a moral person rather than be used as an "object."

The special exceptional circumstances I have in mind are those in which the right to life is overridden by stronger moral or other axiological claims. They may include the protection of the equal rights of others, including others' right to life itself (such as in the case of soldiers sent by their country to war, to defend the lives and freedoms of their countrymen against an aggressor nation); or situations where a certain act is (1) the lesser of two evils and (2) violates no one's equal human or other moral rights, or the principles of fairness and justice. For instance, in some instances of passive or active euthanasia, or assisted suicide, such as in the case of terminal patients who are suffering unbearable physical pain (condition [1]) and the euthanasia or assisted suicide fulfils the patient's devout wish and desire to die (condition [2]). Except in such or similar exceptional cases, the deliberate or the knowing killing of innocent persons is morally wrong.

Elsewhere[41] I have argued that we must acknowledge a fundamental human right of all individuals to be treated as moral persons. Further, that that right includes an equal right of all to be free to satisfy their needs and interests, and to

actualize their potentials: that is, to seek to realize themselves and their well-being.[42] In addition, I have argued that all human beings have an equal right to equal opportunity and treatment, to help enable them to realize the aforementioned values, either as part of or as implied by the right to be treated as a moral person.

A universal negative human right to life,[43] hence a right to one's physical and mental security and integrity, can be readily derived from the right to equal treatment and opportunity as a premise, if such a right is acknowledged,[44] as a condition of the very possibility of exercising that right at all or any other moral, legal, or other kind of right or rights, including the right to be treated as a moral person as a whole. The rights to equal treatment and opportunity would be empty or meaningless in practice if not in theory if one's security is not protected. Indeed, given Thomas Hobbes' three principal causes of quarrel in human nature—competition, "diffidence" or desire for safety, and the desire for glory in the absence of the protective norm of the equal human right to life and its reinforcement by law, human existence would tend to exemplify Hobbes' State of Nature. There would be "no arts; no letters; no society; and which is worst of all, continual fear, and danger of violent death; and life of man, solitary, poor, nasty, brutish, and short."[45]

---

42 Khatchadourian, "The Human Right," passim.

43 As distinguished from a positive human right to life, which includes—over and above the right not to be physically hurt or killed—a right to a minimum standard of welfare.

44 Such a right can also be derived from John Rawls' first and second principles of justice in *A Theory of Justice* (Cambridge, MA, 1971). *Indeed, the right to equal opportunity is part of his first principle.*

45 Thomas Hobbes, "Self-Interest," in *Great Traditions in Ethics*, 5th ed., Ethel M. Albert et al., eds. (Belmont, CA, 1984), 134. Reprinted from *Leviathan*. I should add that Hobbes himself regarded self-preservation as the first law of (human) nature, and that his social contract, the creation of the "Leviathan" of civil and political society, is intended to provide, inter alia, safety and security.

41 Haig Khatchadourian, "Toward a Foundation for Human Rights," *Man and World,* 18 (1985): 219–240, and "The Human Right to be Treated as a Person," *Journal of Value Inquiry,* 19 (1985): 183–195.

It is clear that if a negative right to life is assumed, terrorists' killings of their immediate victims—unless they satisfy conditions (1) and (2) above—are always morally wrong. In reality, condition (1) may perhaps be sometimes satisfied, but condition (2) cannot ever be satisfied. In fact all types and forms of terrorism I have distinguished seriously violate the human rights of their immediate victims and the victimized as moral persons.

Treating people as moral persons means treating them with consideration in two closely related ways. First, it means respecting their autonomy as individuals with their own desires and interests, plans and projects, commitments and goals. That autonomy is clearly violated if they are humiliated, coerced and terrorized, taken hostage or kidnapped, and above all, killed. Second, consideration involves "a certain cluster of attitudes, hence certain ways of acting toward, reacting to and thinking and feeling about" people.[46] It includes sensitivity to and consideration of their feelings and desires, aspirations, projects, and goals. That in turn is an integral part of treating their life as a whole— including their relationships and memories—as a thing of value. Finally, it includes respecting their "culture or ethnic, religious or racial identity or heritage."[47] These things are the very antithesis of what terrorism does to its victims and the victimized.

In sum, terrorism in general violates both aspects of its targets' right to be treated as moral persons. In retaliatory and moralistic/ religious terrorism, that is no less true of those victims or those victimized who are morally responsible in some degree for the wrong that precipitates the terrorist strike than of those who are completely innocent of it. In predatory terrorism, the terrorist acts violate the human right of everyone directly or indirectly hurt by them. For the terrorists

the life of the immediate victims and their human rights matter not in the least. The same goes for the victimized. The terrorists use both groups, against their will, simply as means to their own end.[48] The matter can also be looked upon in terms of the ordinary concepts of *justice* and *injustice*. Terror directed against innocent persons is a grave injustice against them. In no case is this truer than when terrorists impute to their immediate victims or to the victimized guilt by association. It is equally true when the victims are representatives of a government one or more of whose predecessors committed large-scale atrocities, such as attempted genocide, against terrorists' compatriots or ancestors. True, the present government would be tainted by the original crimes if, to cite an actual case, it categorically refuses to acknowledge its predecessors' guilt and take any steps to redress the grievous wrongs. Similarly, if it verbally acknowledges its predecessors' guilt but washes its hands of all moral or legal responsibility to make amends to the survivors of the atrocities or their families, on the ground that it is a new government, existing decades later than the perpetrators. Yet only if the targeted representatives of the present government themselves are in some way responsible for their government's stand would they be noninnocent in some degree. Otherwise targeting them from a desire for revenge would be sheer murder or attempted murder.

Whenever the victims or victimized are innocent persons, terrorism directed against them constitutes a very grave injustice, like "punishing" an innocent person for a crime he or she has not committed. For in the present sense, justice consists in one's receiving what one merits or

---

46 Khatchadourian, "The Human Right," 192.
47 Ibid.

48 Cf. Abraham Edel's condemnation of terrorism on Kant's principle that "people ought to be treated as ends in themselves and never as means only. Terrorists necessarily treat human beings as means to the achievement of their political, economic, or social goals." Quoted by Burton M. Leiser in his introduction to the section on terrorism in his *Values in Conflict* (New York, 1981), 343.

deserves, determined by what one has done or refrained from doing.

It may be argued that some terrorist acts *may* be just punishment for wrongs committed by the immediate victims or the victimized themselves, against the terrorists or persons close to them. But first, punishment cannot be just if founded on a denial of the wrongdoer's human as well as other rights. Second, a vast difference exists between terrorist "punishment" and just legal punishment, which presupposes the establishment of guilt by a preponderance of the evidence. By definition, terrorists do not and cannot respect the legal protections and rights of the victims and the victimized, but erect themselves as judges and jury—and executioners—giving the "accused" no opportunity to defend themselves or be defended by counsel against the terrorists' allegations, let alone the possibility of defending themselves physically against their assailants.[49] This is a further corollary of the terrorists' denial of the moral and legal rights of the victims and victimized.

These strictures apply equally to terrorism from above and from below. The fact that in the former case the terrorist "organization" is the government itself or some arm of government (e.g., its secret police), and that the terrorism is practiced against those of its own citizens it considers dangerous or subversive, does not morally change the situation. It is terrorism by any other name. Such for instance was the situation in Brazil (in the 1960s), Argentina (in the 1970s), Colombia (in the 1980s), and in other Latin American countries when right-wing, anticommunist death squads killed or executed thousands of people suspected of leftist sympathies. In some countries "church and human rights organizations have been particularly hard-hit."[50]

To sum up. The discussion of the nature of terrorism prepared the way for the central question: whether terrorism is ever morally right, morally justifiable. To answer that question two kinds of ethical principles/rules were deployed, (A) applicable human rights, and (B) applicable just war principles/rules. . . . On both (A) and (B), terrorism in general, in all its various types and forms, was found to be always wrong.

Since predatory and retaliatory terrorism, like predation and retaliation in general, are patently wrong, the inquiry was focused on political and moralistic/religious terrorism, which are held by some—with apparent plausibility—to be, in certain circumstances, morally justifiable. However, it was argued that terrorism of both types is wrong, since both violate certain basic human rights and applicable just war principles or rules.

49 See Haig Khatchadourian, "Is Political Assassination Ever Morally Justified?" in *Assassination,* Harold Zellner, ed. (Boston, 1975), 41–55, for similar criticism of political assassination.

50 Leonard B. Weinberg and Paul B. Davis, *Introduction to Political Terrorism* (New York, 1989), 72.

Review Questions

1. How do Lackey, Regan, and Leiser define terrorism? What objections does Khatchadourian make to these definitions?
2. According to Khatchadourian, what are the five elements of terrorism?
3. What is the core meaning of terrorism, according to Khatchadourian? What distinguishes terrorism from all other uses of force or coercion?
4. Khatchadourian argues that three principles of just war theory are flagrantly violated by terrorism. What are these three principles, and why does terrorism violate them?

5. In addition, Khatchadourian argues that all but the moralistic/religious type of terrorism violate a further condition of just war theory. What is this condition and why does terrorism violate it?
6. How does Khatchadourian explain the right to life? When can this right be overridden?
7. Khatchadourian argues that terrorism violates basic human rights. What are these rights and why does terrorism violate them?

Discussion Questions

1. Does Khatchadourian succeed in proving that "terrorism, in all its types and forms, is always wrong"? For example, what about acts of terrorism by Jews in Germany during World War II?
2. The bombing of Hiroshima and Nagasaki caused the death of over 200,000 noncombatants. Was this an act of terrorism? If so, was it morally wrong? Explain your answers.
3. Given Khatchadourian's account of innocence and noninnocence, is anyone perfectly innocent? Who has no share in the moral responsibility, no causal responsibility at all, for any wrong that gives or gave rise to terrorism?

The Terrorist's Tacit Message*

LAURIE CALHOUN

Laurie Calhoun is the author of *Philosophy Unmasked: A Skeptic's Critique* (1997) and many essays on ethics, rhetoric, and war.

Like Khatchadourian in the previous reading, Calhoun applies just war theory to terrorism. Terrorism is condemned by the governments of democratic nations, who continue to engage in "just wars." But when the assumptions involved in the "just war" approach to group conflict are examined, it emerges that terrorists merely follow these assumptions to their logical conclusion. They see themselves fighting "just wars," as "warriors for justice." That is their tacit message. Accordingly, unless the stance toward war embraced by most governments of the world transforms radically, terrorism can be expected to continue over time. As groups proliferate, so will conflicts, and some groups will resort to deadly force, reasoning along "just war" lines. Because terrorists are innovative strategists, it is doubtful that measures based upon conventional military operations will effectively counter terrorism.

Source: Reprinted from *The Peace Review*. © Taylor & Francis Ltd. Used by permission of the publisher. http://www.tandf.co.uk/journals
*Editor's Note: This article was written before 9/11.

THE REFUSAL TO "negotiate with terrorists" is a common refrain in political parlance. It is often accepted as self-evident that terrorists are so far beyond the pale that it would be morally reprehensible even to engage in discourse with them. But the term "terrorist" remains elusive, defined in various ways by various parties, albeit always derogatorily. Judging from the use of the term by the government officials of disparate nations, it would seem to be analytically true that, whoever the speakers may be, they are not terrorists. "Terrorists" refers exclusively to *them,* a lesser or greater set of political actors, depending ultimately upon the sympathies of the speaker.

Government leaders often speak as though terrorists are beyond the reach of reason, but particular terrorists in particular places believe that they are transmitting to the populace a message with concrete content. The message invariably takes the following general form: *There is something seriously wrong with the world in which we live, and this must be changed.* Terrorists sometimes claim to have as their aim to rouse the populace to consciousness so that they might at last see what the terrorists take themselves to have seen. However, the members of various terrorist groups together transmit (unwittingly) a more global message. The lesson that we ought to glean from terrorists is not the specific, context-dependent message that they hope through their use of violence to convey. Terrorists are right that there is something seriously wrong with the world in which we and they live, but they are no less a party to the problem than are the governments against which they inveigh.

That the annihilation of human life is sometimes morally permissible or even obligatory is embodied in two social practices: the execution of criminals and the maintenance of military institutions. This suggests that there are two distinct ways of understanding terrorists' interpretations of their own actions. Either they are attempting to effect "vigilante justice," or else they are fighting "just wars." Because their victims are typically non-combatants, terrorist actions more closely resemble acts of war than vigilante killings. There are of course killers who do not conceive of their own crimes along these lines, having themselves no political agenda or moral mission. Unfortunately, the tendency of governments to conflate terrorists with ordinary murderers (without political agendas) shrouds the similarity between the violent activities of factional groups and those of formal nations.

Attempts to identify "terrorists" by appeal to what these people do give rise to what some might find to be embarrassing implications. For example, to specify "terrorism" as necessarily *illegal* leads to problems in interpreting the reign of terror imposed by The Third Reich in Nazi Germany and other governmental regimes of ill repute. One might, then, propose a moral rather than a legal basis, for example, by delineating "terrorists" as *ideologically or politically motivated actors who kill or threaten to kill innocent people bearing no responsibility for the grievances of the killers.* This would imply that every nation that has engaged in bombing campaigns resulting in the deaths of innocent children has committed acts of terrorism. Faced with this proposed assimilation of nations and factions that deploy deadly force, most people will simply back away, insisting that, though a precise definition is not possible, certain obvious examples of terrorists can be enumerated, and so "terrorist" can be defined by ostension.

The governments of democratic nations harshly condemn "terrorists," but when the assumptions involved in any view according to which war is sometimes just are carefully examined, it emerges that terrorists merely follow these assumptions to their logical conclusion, given the situations in which they find themselves. While nations prohibit the use of deadly force by individuals and sub-national factions, in fact, violent attacks upon strategic targets can be understood straightforwardly as permitted by "just war" rationales, at least as interpreted by the killers. Small terrorist groups could not, with any chance of success, attack a formal military institution, so instead they select targets for their shock appeal.

While secrecy is often thought to be of the very essence of terrorism, the covert practices of terrorist groups are due in part to their illegality. The members of such groups often hide their identities (or at least their own involvement in particular acts of terrorism), not because they believe that their actions are wrong, but because it would be imprudent to expose themselves. Clearly, if one is subject to arrest for publicly committing an act, then one's efficacy as a soldier for the cause in question will be short-lived. Committing illegal acts in the open renders an actor immediately vulnerable to arrest and incarceration, but it is precisely because factional groups reject the legitimacy of the reigning regime that they undertake secretive initiatives best understood as militarily strategic. "Intelligence agencies" are an important part of modern military institutions, and secrecy has long been regarded as integral to martial excellence. Sun Tzu, author of the ancient Chinese classic *The Art of War,* observed nearly three thousand years ago that "All warfare is based on deception."

It is perhaps often simply terrorists' fervent commitment to their cause that leads them to maximize the efficacy of their campaigns by sheltering themselves from vulnerability to the laws of the land, as any prudent transgressor of the law would do. At the other extreme, suicide missions, in which agents openly act in ways that lead to their personal demise, are undertaken only when such martyrdom appears to be the most effective means of drawing attention to the cause. Far from being beyond rational comprehension, the actions of terrorists are dictated by military strategy deployed in the name of what the actors believe to be justice. The extreme lengths to which terrorists are willing to go, the sacrifices that they will make in their efforts to effect a change in the *status quo,* evidence their ardent commitment to their cause.

The common construal of war as a sometimes "necessary evil" implies that war may be waged when the alternative (not waging war) would be worse. If the military could have achieved its objectives without killing innocent people, then it would have done so. Military spokesmen have often maintained that unintended civilian deaths, even when foreseen, are permissible, provided the situation is sufficiently grave. In the just war tradition, what matters, morally speaking, is whether such "collateral damage" is intended by the actors. Equally integral to defenses of the moral permissibility of collateral damage is the principle of last resort, according to which non-belligerent means must have been attempted and failed. If war is not a last resort, then collateral damage is avoidable and therefore morally impermissible. Few would deny that, if there exist ways to resolve a conflict without destroying innocent persons in the process, then those methods must, morally speaking, be pursued. But disputes arise, in specific contexts, regarding whether in fact non-belligerent means to conflict resolution exist. To say that during wartime people *resort* to deadly force is to say that they have a reason, for it is of the very nature of justification to advert to reasons. Defenders of the recourse by nations to deadly force as a means of conflict resolution are willing to condone the killing of innocent people under certain circumstances. The question becomes: When have non-belligerent means been exhausted?

Perhaps the most important (though seldom acknowledged) problem with just war theory is its inextricable dependence upon the interpretation of the very people considering recourse to deadly force. Human fallibility is a given, so in owning that war is justified in some cases, one must acknowledge that the "facts" upon which a given interpretation is based may prove to be false. And anyone who affirms the right (or obligation) to wage war when *they believe* the tenets of just war theory to be satisfied, must, in consistency, also affirm this right (or obligation) for all those who find themselves in analogous situations. But throughout human history wars have been characterized by their instigators as "just," including those retrospectively denounced as grossly unjust, for example, Hitler's campaign. People tend to ascribe good intentions to their own leaders and comrades while ascribing evil intentions to those stigmatized by officials as "the enemy."

The simplicity of its intuitive principles accounts for the widespread appeal of the "just war" paradigm. Throughout human history appeals to principles of "just cause" and "last resort" have been made by both sides to virtually every violent conflict. "Just war" rationalizations are available to everyone, Hussein as well as Bush, Milosevic as well as Clinton. To take a recent example, we find Timothy McVeigh characterizing the deaths of innocent people in the Oklahoma City bombing as "collateral damage." The public response to McVeigh's "preposterous" appropriation of just war theory suggests how difficult it is for military supporters to admit that they are not so very different from the political killers whose actions they condemn.

The received view is that the intention of planting bombs in public places such as the Federal Building in Oklahoma City or the World Trade Center in New York City is to terrorize, and the people who do such things are terrorists. According to the received view, though some innocent people may have been traumatized and killed during the Vietnam War, the Gulf War, and NATO's 1999 bombing campaign in Kosovo, whatever the intentions behind those actions may have been, they certainly were not to *terrorize* people. Nations excuse as regrettable though unavoidable the deaths of children such as occurred during the Gulf War, the Vietnam War, and in Kosovo during NATO's bombing campaign against the regime of Slobodan Milosevic. "Terrorists" are the people who threaten or deploy deadly force for causes of which we do not approve.

Political organizations have often engaged in actions intended to instill fear in the populace and thus draw attention to their cause. But the groups that engage in what is typically labeled "terrorism" are motivated by grievances no less than are nations engaged in war. Were their grievances somehow alleviated, dissenting political groups would no longer feel the need to engage in what they interpret to be "just wars." In appropriating military rationales and tactics, terrorists underscore the obvious, that nations are conventionally assembled groups of people who appoint their leaders just as do sub-national factions. The problem with the received view is that it exercises maximal interpretive charity when it comes to nations (most often, the interpreter's own), while minimal interpretive charity when it comes to sub-national groups. The intention of a terrorist act, *as understood by the terrorist,* is not the immediate act of terrorism, but to air some grave concern, which the terrorist is attempting to bring to the public's attention. In reality, the requirement of "last resort" seems far simpler to fulfill in the cases of smaller, informal factional groups than in those involving a first-world super power such as the United States, the economic policies of which can, with only minor modifications, spell catastrophe for an offending regime. According to the just war tradition, the permissible use of deadly force is a last resort, deployed only after all pacific means have proven infeasible, and the terrorist most likely reasons along precisely these lines. Indeed, the urgency of the terrorist's situation (to his own mind) makes his own claims regarding last resort all the more compelling. A terrorist, no less than the military spokesmen of established nations, may regret the deaths of the innocent people to which his activities give rise. But, applying the "just war" approach to "collateral damage," terrorists may emerge beyond moral reproach, since were their claims adequately addressed by the powers that be, they would presumably cease their violent activities. It is because they believe that their rights have been denied that groups engage in the activities identified as "terrorism" and thought by most people to be morally distinct from the military actions of states.

Once one grants the possibility of a "just war," it seems to follow straightforwardly that political dissidents convinced of the unjust practices of the government in power ought to engage in violent acts of subversion. Factions lack the advantage of currently enshrined institutions that naturally perpetuate the very *status quo* claimed by dissidents to be unjust. Accordingly, so long as nations continue to wage wars in the name of "justice," it seems plausible that smaller groups and factions will do so as well. Many terrorist groups insist that their claims have been squelched or ignored by the regime in power. But if formal nations may wage war to defend their own integrity and sovereignty, then why not separatist groups? And if such a group lacks a nationally funded and sanctioned army, then must not the group assemble its own?

The terrorist is not a peculiar type of creature who nefariously resorts to deadly force in opposition to the demands of morality upheld by all civilized nations. Rather, the terrorist merely embraces the widely held view that deadly military action is morally permissible, while delimiting "nations" differently than do those who uncritically accept the conventions which they have been raised to believe. The nations in existence are historically contingent, not a part of the very essence of things. The terrorist recognizes that current nations came into being and transformed as a result of warfare. Accordingly, agents who, in the name of justice, wield deadly force against the society in which they live conceive of themselves as civil warriors. Terrorist groups are smaller armies than those of established nations funded by taxpayers and sanctioned by the law, but for this very reason they may feel compelled to avail themselves of particularly drastic methods. No less than the military leaders of most countries throughout history, terrorists maintain that the situations which call for war are so desperate as to require the extremest of measures.

That a terrorist is not *sui generis* can be illustrated as follows: Imagine the commander-in-chief of any established nation being, instead, the leader of a group dissenting from the currently reigning regime. The very same person's acts of deadly violence (or his ordering his comrades to commit such acts) do not differ in his own mind merely because he has been formally designated the commander-in-chief in one case but not in the other. Both parties to every conflict maintain that they are right and their adversaries wrong, and terrorist factions are not exceptional in this respect. When we look carefully at the situation of terrorists, it becomes difficult to identify any morally significant distinction between what they do and what formal nations do in flying planes over enemy nations and dropping bombs, knowing full well that innocent people will die as a result of their actions.

Most advanced nations with standing armies not only produce but also export the types of deadly weapons used by factions in terrorist actions. If we restrict the use of the term "terrorist" to those groups that deploy deadly violence "beyond the pale" of any established legal system, then it follows that terrorists derive their weapons from more formal (and legal) military institutions and industries. The conventional weapons trade has proven all but impossible to control, given the ease with which stockpiled arms are transferred from regime to regime and provided by some countries to smaller groups that they deem to be politically correct. And even when scandals such as Iran-Contra are brought to light, seldom are the culpable agents held more than nominally accountable for their actions. Leniency toward military personnel and political leaders who engage in or facilitate patriotic though illegal weapons commerce results from the basic assumption on the part of most people, that they and their comrades are good, while those who disagree are not.

In some cases, terrorists develop innovative weapons through the use of materials with non-military applications, for example, sulfuric acid or ammonium nitrate. Given the possibility for innovative destruction by terrorist groups, it would seem that even more instrumental to the perpetuation of terrorism than the ongoing exportation of deadly weapons is the support by national leaders of *the idea* that killing human beings can be a mandate of justice. Bombing campaigns serve as graphic illustrations of the approbation by governments of the use of deadly force. It is simple indeed to understand what must be a common refrain among members of dissenting groups who adopt violent means: "If they can do it, then why cannot we?"

Political groups have agendas, and some of these groups deploy violence strategically in attempting to effect their aims. Terrorists are not "beyond the pale," intellectually and morally speaking, for their actions are best understood through appeal to the very just war theory invoked by nations in defending their own military campaigns. Terrorists interpret their own wars as just, while holding culpable all those who benefit from the policies of the government with which they disagree. The groups commonly identified as "terrorists" disagree with governments about not whether there can be a just war, nor whether morality is of such paramount importance as sometimes to require the killing of innocent people. Terrorist groups and the military institutions of nations embrace the very same "just war" schema, disagreeing only about facts.

Thus we find that the terrorist conveys two distinct messages. First, and this is usually the only claim to truth recognized by outsiders, the terrorist alleges injustices within the framework of society. In many cases there may be some truth to the specific charges made by terrorist groups, and this would be enough to turn against them all those who benefit from the regime in power. But a second and more important type of truth is highlighted by the very conduct of the terrorist. Perhaps there is something profoundly misguided about not only some of the specific policies within our societies, but also the manner in which we conceptualize the institutionalized use of deadly force, the activity of war, as an acceptable route to dispute resolution.

The connotations associated with "terrorist" are strongly pejorative and, although terrorists clearly operate from within what they take to be a moral framework, they are often subject to much more powerful condemnation than non-political killers. But murderers who reject the very idea of morality would seem to be worse enemies of society than are political terrorists, who are motivated primarily by moral considerations. Why is it, then, that people fear and loathe terrorists so intensely? Perhaps they recognize, on some level, that terrorists are operating along lines that society in fact implicitly condones and even encourages. Perhaps people see shadows of themselves and their own activities in those of terrorists.

If it is true that terrorists view themselves as warriors for justice, then unless the stance toward war embraced by most governments of the world transforms radically, terrorism should be expected to continue over time. To the extent to which groups proliferate, conflicts will as well, and some subset of the parties to conflict will resort to deadly force, buoyed by what they, along with most of the populace, take to be the respectability of "just war." Military solutions are no longer used even by stable nations merely as "last resorts." Tragically, the ready availability of deadly weapons and the widespread assumption that the use of such weapons is often morally acceptable, if not obligatory, has brought about a world in which leaders often think first, not last, of military solutions to conflict. This readiness to deploy deadly means has arguably contributed to the escalation of violence in the contemporary world on many different levels, the most frightening of which being to many people those involving the unpredictable actions of factional groups, "the terrorists." But the leaders of established nations delude themselves in thinking that they will quell terrorism through threats and weapons proliferation. Terrorists "innovate" by re-defining what are commonly thought of as non-military targets as military. There is no reason for believing that terrorists' capacity for innovation will be frustrated by the construction of an anti-ballistic missile system or the implementation of other initiatives premised upon conventional military practices and strategies.

Recommended Readings

Arendt, Hannah. 1979. *The Origins of Totalitarianism*. New York: Harcourt Brace.

Calhoun, Laurie. 2002. "How Violence Breeds Violence: Some Utilitarian Considerations," *Politics*, vol. 22, no. 2, pp. 95–108.

Calhoun, Laurie. 2001. "Killing, Letting Die, and the Alleged Necessity of Military Intervention," *Peace and Conflict Studies*, vol. 8, no. 2, pp. 5–22.

Calhoun, Laurie. 2001. "The Metaethical Paradox of Just War Theory," *Ethical Theory and Moral Practice*, vol. 4, no. 1, pp. 41–58.

Calhoun, Laurie. 2002. "The Phenomenology of Paid Killing," *International Journal of Human Rights*, vol. 6, no. 1, pp. 1–18.

Calhoun, Laurie. 2001. "Violence and Hypocrisy," and "Laurie Calhoun replies [to Michael Walzer]," *Dissent*, (winter) vol. 48, no. 1 pp. 79–87. Reprinted in *Just War: A Casebook in Argumentation*, eds. Walsh & Asch, Heinle/Thomson, 2004.

Cerovic, Stanko. 2001. *Dans les griffes des humanistes*, trans. Mireille Robin. Paris: Éditions Climats.

Colson, Bruno. 1999. *L'art de la guerre de Machiavel à Clausewitz*. Namur: Bibliothèque Universitaire Moretus Plantin.

Cooper, H. H. A. 2001. "Terrorism: The Problem of Definition Revisited," *American Behavioral Scientist*, vol. 44, no. 6, pp. 881–893.

Gibbs, Jack P. 1989. "Conceptualization of Terrorism," *American Sociological Review*, vol. 54, no. 3, pp. 329–340.

Grossman, Lt. Colonel Dave. 1995. *On Killing: The Psychological Cost of Learning to Kill in War and Society*. Boston: Little Brown.

Harman, Gilbert. 2000. *Explaining Value*. Oxford: Oxford University Press.

Harman, Gilbert. 1977. *The Nature of Morality*. New York: Oxford University Press.

Holmes, Robert L. 1989. *On War and Morality*. Princeton: Princeton University Press.

Le Borgne, Claude. 1986. *La Guerre est Morte . . . mais on ne le sait pas encore*. Paris: Bernard Grasset.

Rapoport, David C. 1984. "Fear and Trembling: Terrorism in Three Religious Traditions," *The American Political Science Review*, vol. 78, no. 3, pp. 658–677.

Review Questions

1. According to Calhoun, what is the concrete message of terrorists? What is the more global message, the "tacit message"?
2. What problems does Calhoun see with the legal and moral definitions of "terrorists"?
3. How do terrorists view their actions, according to Calhoun?
4. How do military spokesmen justify "collateral damage," or the killing of innocent people, according to Calhoun?
5. What role does interpretation play in just war theory, in Calhoun's view? Why does she think that "just war" rationalizations are available to everyone, from Hussein to Bush?
6. According to Calhoun, what is the intention of the terrorist act, as understood by the terrorist?
7. Why does Calhoun believe that terrorism is best understood by appealing to the very just war theory invoked by nations defending their wars?

Discussion Questions

1. Calhoun argues that anyone can rationalize war or terrorism by appealing to just war theory. Is this true or not? Why or why not?

2. Calhoun says: "Terrorists are people who threaten or deploy deadly force for causes of which we do not approve." Do you agree? Why or why not?
3. Calhoun claims that there is hardly any moral difference between what the terrorists do and what nations such as the United States do when they drop bombs on enemy nations knowing full well that innocent people will die. Do you agree? Why or why not?

The War on Terrorism and the End of Human Rights

DAVID LUBAN

David Luban is the Frederick J. Hass Professor of Law and Philosophy at the Georgetown University Law Center. He is the author of *Lawyers and Justice* (1988), *Legal Modernism* (1994), and numerous journal articles and book chapters.

Luban argues that the current War on Terrorism combines a war model with a law model to produce a new model of state action, a hybrid war-law model. This hybrid model selectively picks out elements of the war and law models to maximize the use of lethal force while eliminating the rights of both adversaries and innocent bystanders. The result is that the War on Terrorism means the end of human rights.

IN THE IMMEDIATE aftermath of September 11, President Bush stated that the perpetrators of the deed would be brought to justice. Soon afterwards, the President announced that the United States would engage in a war on terrorism. The first of these statements adopts the familiar language of criminal law and criminal justice. It treats the September 11 attacks as horrific crimes—mass murders—and the government's mission as apprehending and punishing the surviving planners and conspirators for their roles in the crimes. The War on Terrorism is a different proposition, however, and a different model of governmental action—not law but war. Most

Source: Luban, David, "The War on Terrorism and the End of Human Rights," from *Philosophy & Public Policy Quarterly*, Vol. 22, No. 3 (Summer 2002). Reprinted by permission of Rowman and Littlefield Publishing Group.

obviously, it dramatically broadens the scope of action, because now terrorists who knew nothing about September 11 have been earmarked as enemies. But that is only the beginning.

THE HYBRID WAR-LAW APPROACH

The model of war offers much freer rein than that of law, and therein lies its appeal in the wake of 9/11. First, in war but not in law it is permissible to use lethal force on enemy troops regardless of their degree of personal involvement with the adversary. The conscripted cook is as legitimate a target as the enemy general. Second, in war but not in law "collateral damage," that is, foreseen but unintended killing of noncombatants, is permissible. (Police cannot blow up an apartment building full of people because a murderer is inside, but an air force can bomb the building if it contains a military target.) Third, the requirements of evidence and proof are drastically weaker in war than in criminal justice. Soldiers do not need proof beyond a reasonable doubt, or even proof by a preponderance of evidence, that someone is an enemy soldier before firing on him or capturing and imprisoning him. They don't need proof at all, merely plausible intelligence. Thus, the U.S. military remains regretful but unapologetic about its January 2002 attack on the Afghani town of Uruzgan, in which 21 innocent civilians were killed, based on faulty intelligence that they were al Qaeda fighters. Fourth, in war one can attack an enemy without concern over whether he has done anything. Legitimate targets are those who in the course of combat *might* harm us, not those who *have* harmed us. No doubt there are other significant differences as well. But the basic point should be clear: Given Washington's mandate to eliminate the danger of future 9/11s, so far as humanly possible, the model of war offers important advantages over the model of law.

There are disadvantages as well. Most obviously, in war but not in law, fighting back is a *legitimate* response of the enemy. Second, when nations fight a war, other nations may opt for neutrality. Third, because fighting back is legitimate, in war the enemy soldier deserves special regard once he is rendered harmless through injury or surrender. It is impermissible to punish him for his role in fighting the war. Nor can he be harshly interrogated after he is captured. The Third Geneva Convention provides: "Prisoners of war who refuse to answer [questions] may not be threatened, insulted, or exposed to unpleasant or disadvantageous treatment of any kind." And, when the war concludes, the enemy soldier must be repatriated.

Here, however, Washington has different ideas, designed to eliminate these tactical disadvantages in the traditional war model. Washington regards international terrorism not only as a military adversary, but also as a criminal activity and criminal conspiracy. In the law model, criminals don't get to shoot back, and their acts of violence subject them to legitimate punishment. That is what we see in Washington's prosecution of the War on Terrorism. Captured terrorists may be tried before military or civilian tribunals, and shooting back at Americans, including American troops, is a federal crime (for a statute under which John Walker Lindh was indicted criminalizes anyone regardless of nationality, who "outside the United States attempts to kill, or engages in a conspiracy to kill, a national of the United States" or "engages in physical violence with intent to cause serious bodily injury to a national of the United States; or with the result that serious bodily injury is caused to a national of the United States"). Furthermore, the U.S. may rightly demand that other countries not be neutral about murder and terrorism. Unlike the war model, a nation may insist that those who are not with us in fighting murder and terror are against us, because by not joining our operations they are providing a safe haven for terrorists or their bank accounts. By selectively combining elements of the war model and elements of the law model, Washington is able to maximize its own ability to mobilize lethal force against terrorists while eliminating most traditional rights of a military adversary, as well as the rights of innocent bystanders caught in the crossfire.

A LIMBO OF RIGHTLESSNESS

The legal status of al Qaeda suspects imprisoned at the Guantanamo Bay Naval Base in Cuba is emblematic of this hybrid war-law approach to the threat of terrorism. In line with the war model, they lack the usual rights of criminal suspects—the presumption of innocence, the right to a hearing to determine guilt, the opportunity to prove that the authorities have grabbed the wrong man. But, in line with the law model, they are considered *unlawful* combatants. Because they are not uniformed forces, they lack the rights of prisoners of war and are liable to criminal punishment. Initially, the

American government declared that the Guantanamo Bay prisoners have no rights under the Geneva Conventions. In the face of international protests, Washington quickly backpedaled and announced that the Guantanamo Bay prisoners would indeed be treated as decently as POWs—but it also made clear that the prisoners have no right to such treatment. Neither criminal suspects nor POWs, neither fish nor fowl, they inhabit a limbo of rightlessness. Secretary of Defense Rumsfeld's assertion that the U.S. may continue to detain them even if they are acquitted by a military tribunal dramatizes the point.

To understand how extraordinary their status is, consider an analogy. Suppose that Washington declares a War on Organized Crime. Troops are dispatched to Sicily, and a number of Mafiosi are seized, brought to Guantanamo Bay, and imprisoned without a hearing for the indefinite future, maybe the rest of their lives. They are accused of no crimes, because their capture is based not on what they have done but on what they might do. After all, to become "made" they took oaths of obedience to the bad guys. Seizing them accords with the war model: they are enemy foot soldiers. But they are foot soldiers out of uniform; they lack a "fixed distinctive emblem," in the words of The Hague Convention. That makes them unlawful combatants, so they lack the rights of POWs. They may object that it is only a unilateral declaration by the American President that has turned them into combatants in the first place—he called it a war, they didn't—and that, since they do not regard themselves as literal foot soldiers it never occurred to them to wear a fixed distinctive emblem. They have a point. It seems too easy for the President to divest anyone in the world of rights and liberty simply by announcing that the U.S. is at war with them and then declaring them unlawful combatants if they resist. But, in the hybrid war-law model, they protest in vain.

Consider another example. In January 2002, U.S. forces in Bosnia seized five Algerians and a Yemeni suspected of al Qaeda connections and took them to Guantanamo Bay. The six had been jailed in Bosnia, but a Bosnian court released

them for lack of evidence, and the Bosnian Human Rights Chamber issued an injunction that four of them be allowed to remain in the country pending further legal proceedings. The Human Rights Chamber, ironically, was created under U.S. auspices in the Dayton peace accords, and it was designed specifically to protect against treatment like this. Ruth Wedgwood, a well-known international law scholar at Yale and a member of the Council on Foreign Relations, defended the Bosnian seizure in war-model terms. "I think we would simply argue this was a matter of self-defense. One of the fundamental rules of military law is that you have a right ultimately to act in self-defense. And if these folks were actively plotting to blow up the U.S. embassy, they should be considered combatants and captured as combatants in a war." Notice that Professor Wedgwood argues in terms of what the men seized in Bosnia were *planning to do,* not what they *did;* notice as well that the decision of the Bosnian court that there was insufficient evidence does not matter. These are characteristics of the war model.

More recently, two American citizens alleged to be al Qaeda operatives (Jose Padilla, a.k.a. Abdullah al Muhajir, and Yasser Esam Hamdi) have been held in American military prisons, with no crimes charged, no opportunity to consult counsel, and no hearing. The President described Padilla as "a bad man" who aimed to build a nuclear "dirty" bomb and use it against America; and the Justice Department has classified both men as "enemy combatants" who may be held indefinitely. Yet, as military law expert Gary Solis points out, "Until now, as used by the attorney general, the term 'enemy combatant' appeared nowhere in U.S. criminal law, international law or in the law of war." The phrase comes from the 1942 Supreme Court case *Ex parte Quirin,* but all the Court says there is that "an enemy combatant who without uniform comes secretly through the lines for the purpose of waging war by destruction of life or property" would "not . . . be entitled to the status of prisoner of war, but . . . [they would] be offenders against the law of war subject to trial and punishment by military tribunals." For the Court, in other words, the status of a person as a non-uniformed enemy combatant makes him a criminal rather than a warrior, and determines *where* he is tried (in a military, rather than a civilian, tribunal) but not *whether* he is tried. Far from authorizing open-ended confinement, *Ex parte Quirin* presupposes that criminals are entitled to hearings: without a hearing how can suspects prove that the government made a mistake? *Quirin* embeds the concept of "enemy combatant" firmly in the law model. In the war model, by contrast, POWs may be detained without a hearing until hostilities are over. But POWs were captured in uniform, and only their undoubted identity as enemy soldiers justifies such open-ended custody. Apparently, Hamdi and Padilla will get the worst of both models—open-ended custody with no trial, like POWs, but no certainty beyond the U.S. government's say-so that they really are "bad men." This is the hybrid war-law model. It combines the *Quirin* category of "enemy combatant without uniform," used in the law model to justify a military trial, with the war model's practice of indefinite confinement with no trial at all.

THE CASE FOR THE HYBRID APPROACH

Is there any justification for the hybrid war-law model, which so drastically diminishes the rights of the enemy? An argument can be offered along the following lines. In ordinary cases of war among states, enemy soldiers may well be morally and politically innocent. Many of them are conscripts, and those who aren't do not necessarily endorse the state policies they are fighting to defend. But enemy soldiers in the War on Terrorism are, by definition, those who have embarked on a path of terrorism. They are neither morally nor politically innocent. Their sworn aim—"Death to America!"—is to create more 9/11s. In this respect, they are much more akin to criminal conspirators than to

conscript soldiers. Terrorists will fight as soldiers when they must, and metamorphose into mass murderers when they can.

Furthermore, suicide terrorists pose a special, unique danger. Ordinary criminals do not target innocent bystanders. They may be willing to kill them if necessary, but bystanders enjoy at least some measure of security because they are not primary targets. Not so with terrorists, who aim to kill as many innocent people as possible. Likewise, innocent bystanders are protected from ordinary criminals by whatever deterrent force the threat of punishment and the risk of getting killed in the act of committing a crime offer. For a suicide bomber, neither of these threats is a deterrent at all—after all, for the suicide bomber one of the hallmarks of a *successful* operation is that he winds up dead at day's end. Given the unique and heightened danger that suicide terrorists pose, a stronger response that grants potential terrorists fewer rights may be justified. Add to this the danger that terrorists may come to possess weapons of mass destruction, including nuclear devices in suitcases. Under circumstances of such dire menace, it is appropriate to treat terrorists as though they embody the most dangerous aspects of both warriors and criminals. That is the basis of the hybrid war-law model.

THE CASE AGAINST EXPEDIENCY

The argument against the hybrid war-law model is equally clear. The U.S. has simply chosen the bits of the law model and the bits of the war model that are most convenient for American interests, and ignored the rest. The model abolishes the rights of potential enemies (and their innocent shields) by fiat—not for reasons of moral or legal principle, but solely because the U.S. does not want them to have rights. The more rights they have, the more risk they pose. But Americans' urgent desire to minimize our risks doesn't make other people's rights disappear. Calling our policy a War on Terrorism obscures this point.

The theoretical basis of the objection is that the law model and the war model each comes as a package, with a kind of intellectual integrity. The law model grows out of relationships within states, while the war model arises from relationships between states. The law model imputes a ground-level community of values to those subject to the law—paradigmatically, citizens of a state, but also visitors and foreigners who choose to engage in conduct that affects a state. Only because law imputes shared basic values to the community can a state condemn the conduct of criminals and inflict punishment on them. Criminals deserve condemnation and punishment because their conduct violates norms that we are entitled to count on their sharing. But, for the same reason—the imputed community of values—those subject to the law ordinarily enjoy a presumption of innocence and an expectation of safety. The government cannot simply grab them and confine them without making sure they have broken the law, nor can it condemn them without due process for ensuring that it has the right person, nor can it knowingly place bystanders in mortal peril in the course of fighting crime. They are our fellows, and the community should protect them just as it protects us. The same imputed community of values that justifies condemnation and punishment creates rights to due care and due process.

War is different. War is the ultimate acknowledgment that human beings do not live in a single community with shared norms. If their norms conflict enough, communities pose a physical danger to each other, and nothing can safeguard a community against its enemies except force of arms. That makes enemy soldiers legitimate targets; but it makes our soldiers legitimate targets as well, and, once the enemy no longer poses a danger, he should be immune from punishment, because if he has fought cleanly he has violated no norms that we are entitled to presume he honors. Our norms are, after all, *our* norms, not his.

Because the law model and war model come as conceptual packages, it is unprincipled to wrench them apart and recombine them simply because it is in America's interest to do so. To declare that Americans can fight enemies with the latitude of warriors, but if the enemies fight back they are not warriors but criminals, amounts to a kind of heads-I-win-tails-you-lose international morality in which whatever it takes to reduce American risk, no matter what the cost to others, turns out to be justified. This, in brief, is the criticism of the hybrid war-law model.

To be sure, the law model could be made to incorporate the war model merely by rewriting a handful of statutes. Congress could enact laws permitting imprisonment or execution of persons who pose a significant threat of terrorism whether or not they have already done anything wrong. The standard of evidence could be set low and the requirement of a hearing eliminated. Finally, Congress could authorize the use of lethal force against terrorists regardless of the danger to innocent bystanders, and it could immunize officials from lawsuits or prosecution by victims of collateral damage. Such statutes would violate the Constitution, but the Constitution could be amended to incorporate anti-terrorist exceptions to the Fourth, Fifth, and Sixth Amendments. In the end, we would have a system of law that includes all the essential features of the war model.

It would, however, be a system that imprisons people for their intentions rather than their actions, and that offers the innocent few protections against mistaken detention or inadvertent death through collateral damage. Gone are the principles that people should never be punished for their thoughts, only for their deeds, and that innocent people must be protected rather than injured by their own government. In that sense, at any rate, repackaging war as law seems merely cosmetic, because it replaces the ideal of law as a protector of rights with the more problematic goal of protecting some innocent people by sacrificing others. The hypothetical legislation incorporates war into law only by making law as partisan and ruthless as war. It no longer resembles law as Americans generally understand it.

THE THREAT TO INTERNATIONAL HUMAN RIGHTS

In the War on Terrorism, what becomes of international human rights? It seems beyond dispute that the war model poses a threat to international human rights, because honoring human rights is neither practically possible nor theoretically required during war. Combatants are legitimate targets; non-combatants maimed by accident or mistake are regarded as collateral damage rather than victims of atrocities; cases of mistaken identity get killed or confined without a hearing because combat conditions preclude due process. To be sure, the laws of war specify minimum human rights, but these are far less robust than rights in peacetime—and the hybrid war-law model reduces this schedule of rights even further by classifying the enemy as unlawful combatants.

One striking example of the erosion of human rights is tolerance of torture. It should be recalled that a 1995 al Qaeda plot to bomb eleven U.S. airliners was thwarted by information tortured out of a Pakistani suspect by the Philippine police—an eerie real-life version of the familiar philosophical thought-experiment. The *Washington Post* reports that since September 11 the U.S. has engaged in the summary transfer of dozens of terrorism suspects to countries where they will be interrogated under torture. But it isn't just the United States that has proven willing to tolerate torture for security reasons. Last December, the Swedish government snatched a suspected Islamic extremist to whom it had previously granted political asylum, and the same day had him transferred to Egypt, where Amnesty International reports that he has been tortured to the point where he walks only with difficulty. Sweden is not, to say the least, a traditionally hard-line nation on human rights issues. None of this international transportation is

lawful—indeed, it violates international treaty obligations under the Convention against Torture that in the U.S. have constitutional status as "supreme Law of the Land"—but that may not matter under the war model, in which even constitutional rights may be abrogated.

It is natural to suggest that this suspension of human rights is an exceptional emergency measure to deal with an unprecedented threat. This raises the question of how long human rights will remain suspended. When will the war be over?

Here, the chief problem is that the War on Terrorism is not like any other kind of war. The enemy, Terrorism, is not a territorial state or nation or government. There is no opposite number to negotiate with. There is no one on the other side to call a truce or declare a ceasefire, no one among the enemy authorized to surrender. In traditional wars among states, the war aim is, as Clausewitz argued, to impose one state's political will on another's. The *aim* of the war is not to kill the enemy—killing the enemy is the *means* used to achieve the real end, which is to force capitulation. In the War on Terrorism, no capitulation is possible. That means that the real aim of the war is, quite simply, to kill or capture all of the terrorists—to keep on killing and killing, capturing and capturing, until they are all gone.

Of course, no one expects that terrorism will ever disappear completely. Everyone understands that new anti-American extremists, new terrorists, will always arise and always be available for recruitment and deployment. Everyone understands that even if al Qaeda is destroyed or decapitated, other groups, with other leaders, will arise in its place. It follows, then, that the War on Terrorism will be a war that can only be abandoned, never concluded. The War has no natural resting point, no moment of victory or finality. It requires a mission of killing and capturing, in territories all over the globe, that will go on in perpetuity. It follows as well that the suspension of human rights implicit in the hybrid war-law model is not temporary but permanent.

Perhaps with this fear in mind, Congressional authorization of President Bush's military campaign limits its scope to those responsible for September 11 and their sponsors. But the War on Terrorism has taken on a life of its own that makes the Congressional authorization little more than a technicality. Because of the threat of nuclear terror, the American leadership actively debates a war on Iraq regardless of whether Iraq was implicated in September 11; and the President's yoking of Iraq, Iran, and North Korea into a single axis of evil because they back terror suggests that the War on Terrorism might eventually encompass all these nations. If the U.S. ever unearths tangible evidence that any of these countries is harboring or abetting terrorists with weapons of mass destruction, there can be little doubt that Congress will support military action. So too, Russia invokes the American War on Terrorism to justify its attacks on Chechen rebels, China uses it to deflect criticisms of its campaign against Uighur separatists, and Israeli Prime Minister Sharon explicitly links military actions against Palestinian insurgents to the American War on Terrorism. No doubt there is political opportunism at work in some or all of these efforts to piggy-back onto America's campaign, but the opportunity would not exist if "War on Terrorism" were merely the code-name of a discrete, neatly-boxed American operation. Instead, the War on Terrorism has become a model of politics, a world-view with its own distinctive premises and consequences. As I have argued, it includes a new model of state action, the hybrid war-law model, which depresses human rights from their peace-time standard to the war-time standard, and indeed even further. So long as it continues, the War on Terrorism means the end of human rights, at least for those near enough to be touched by the fire of battle.

Sources: On the January 2002 attack on the Afghani town of Uruzgan, see: John Ward Anderson, "Afghans Falsely Held by U.S. Tried to Explain; Fighters Recount Unanswered Pleas, Beatings—and an Apology on Their Release," *Washington Post* (March 26, 2002); see also Susan B. Glasser, "Afghans Live and Die With U.S. Mistakes; Villagers Tell of Over 100 Casualties," *Washington Post* (Feb. 20, 2002). On the Third Geneva Convention, see: Geneva Convention (III) Relative to the Treatment of Prisoners of War, 6 U.S.T. 3317, signed on August 12, 1949, at Geneva, Article 17. Although the U.S. has not ratified the Geneva Convention, it has become part of customary international law, and certainly belongs to the war model. Count One of the Lindh indictment charges him with violating 18 U.S.C. 2332(b), "Whoever outside the United States attempts to kill, or engages in a conspiracy to kill, a national of the United States" may be sentenced to 20 years (for attempts) or life imprisonment (for conspiracies). Subsection (c) likewise criminalizes "engag[ing] in physical violence with intent to cause serious bodily injury to a national of the United States; or with the result that serious bodily injury is caused to a national of the United States." Lawful combatants are defined in the Hague Convention (IV) Respecting the Laws and Customs of War on Land, Annex to the Convention, 1 Bevans 631, signed on October 18, 1907, at The Hague, Article 1. The definition requires that combatants "have a fixed distinctive emblem recognizable at a distance." Protocol I Additional to the Geneva Conventions of 1949, 1125 U.N.T.S. 3, adopted on June 8, 1977, at Geneva, Article 44(3) makes an important change in the Hague Convention, expanding the definition of combatants to include non-uniformed irregulars. However, the United States has not agreed to Protocol I. The source of Ruth Wedgwood's remarks: Interview with Melissa Block, National Public Radio program, "All Things Considered" (January 18, 2002); Gary Solis, "Even a 'Bad Man' Has Rights," *Washington Post* (June 25, 2002); *Ex parte Quirin*, 317 U.S. 1, 31 (1942). On the torture of the Pakistani militant by Philippine police: Doug Struck et al., "Borderless Network Of Terror; Bin Laden Followers Reach Across Globe," *Washington Post* (September 23, 2001): "'For weeks, agents hit him with a chair and a long piece of wood, forced water into his mouth, and crushed lighted cigarettes into his private parts,' wrote journalists Marites Vitug and Glenda Gloria in 'Under the Crescent Moon,' an acclaimed book on Abu Sayyaf. 'His ribs were almost totally broken and his captors were surprised he survived.'" On U.S. and Swedish transfers of Isamic militants to countries employing torture: Rajiv Chandrasakaran & Peter Finn, "U.S. Behind Secret Transfer of Terror Suspects," *Washington Post* (March 11, 2002); Peter Finn, "Europeans Tossing Terror Suspects Out the Door," *Washington Post* (January 29, 2002); Anthony Shadid, "Fighting Terror/Atmosphere in Europe, Military Campaign/Asylum Bids; in Shift, Sweden Extradites Militants to Egypt," *Boston Globe* (December 31, 2001). Article 3(1) of the Convention against Torture provides that "No State Party shall expel, return ('*refouler*') or extradite a person to another State where there are substantial grounds for believing that he would be in danger of being subjected to torture." Article 2(2) cautions that "No exceptional circumstances whatsoever, whether a state of war or a threat of war, internal political instability or any other public emergency, may be invoked as a justification of torture." But no parallel caution is incorporated into Article 3(1)'s non-*refoulement* rule, and a lawyer might well argue that its

absence implies that the rule may be abrogated during war or similar public emergency. *Convention against Torture and Other Cruel, Inhuman or Degrading Treatment or Punishment,* 1465 U.N.T.S. 85. Ratified by the United States, Oct. 2, 1994. Entered into force for the United States, Nov. 20, 1994. (Article VI of the U.S. Constitution provides that treaties are the "supreme Law of the Land.")

Review Questions

1. According to Luban, what is the traditional model of war? What are its four main features? What are its disadvantages?
2. How does Luban describe the law model? How is it combined with the war model to produce a hybrid war-law approach to terrorism?
3. In Luban's view, what is the legal status of al Qaeda suspects? Do they have any rights?
4. Describe the case of the al Qaeda suspects seized in Bosnia.
5. How does Luban explain the concept of enemy combatant? How is this concept applied to Jose Padilla and Yasser Esam Harudi?
6. According to Luban what is the case for the hybrid war-law model? What is the case against it?
7. In Luban's view, what becomes of human rights in the War on Terrorism?

Discussion Questions

1. In January 2002, the U.S. military killed 21 innocent civilians in an attack on the Afganhi town of Uruzgan. Was this attack justified? Why or why not?
2. Should the Guantanamo prisoners have rights? If so, what are they? If not, why not?
3. Is it acceptable to confine suspected terrorists indefinitely with no trial?
4. Is the hybrid war-law model of the War on Terrorism acceptable? Why or why not?
5. Should torture be used to fight terrorism? Why or why not?

The Concept and Practice of Jihad in Islam

MICHAEL G. KNAPP

Michael G. Knapp is a Middle East/Africa analyst with the U.S. Army National Ground Intelligence Center in Charlottesville, Virginia. He has worked in U.S. government intelligence for over 24 years.

Knapp surveys the development of the concept of jihad in Islam. The classical view was that jihad, defined as fighting in the path of God, was restricted to defensive war against non-Muslims. Modern militant Islam has changed the concept to include

Source: Michael G. Knapp, "The Concept and Practice of Jihad in Islam," from *Parameters,* Spring 2003, pp. 82–94. Used by permission.

wars of aggression against non-Muslims. Now states such as Egypt and its neighbors that mix Islamic and European laws are considered by radicals to be non-Muslim. The radical movement has reached an extreme in the ideology of Osama bin Laden, who has twice declared war, jihad, against the United States and its allies.

"All these crimes and sins committed by the Americans are a clear declaration of war on God, his Messenger, and Muslims. . . . [T]he jihad is an individual duty if the enemy destroys the Muslim countries. . . . As for the fighting to repulse [an enemy], it is aimed at defending sanctity and religion, and it is a duty. . . . On that basis, and in compliance with God's order, we issue the following fatwa to all Muslims: The ruling to kill the Americans and their allies—civilian and military—is an individual duty for every Muslim who can do it in any country in which it is possible to do it."

— Osama bin Laden et al., in "Declaration of the World Islamic Front for Jihad Against the Jews and Crusaders," 23 February 1998

THE WORD "JIHAD" MEANS "struggle" or "striving" (in the way of God) or to work for a noble cause with determination; it does not mean "holy war" (war in Arabic is *harb* and holy is *muqadassa*). Unlike its medieval Christian counterpart term, "crusade" ("war for the cross"), however, the term jihad for Muslims has retained its religious and military connotation into modern times. The word jihad has appeared widely in the Western news media following the 11 September 2001 terrorist attacks on the World Trade Center and the Pentagon, but the true meaning of this term in the Islamic world (it is sometimes called the "sixth pillar" of the faith) is still not well understood by non-Muslims.

In war, the first essential is to know your adversary—how he thinks and why he thinks that way, and what his strategy and objectives are—so that you can attempt to frustrate his plans and protect the lives of your fellow citizens. Understanding how radical Muslims see jihad and are employing it asymmetrically against us can provide us with that kind of perspective.

This article will trace the development of jihad through early Islamic history into the present day, and will focus on how jihad in concept and practice has been appropriated and distorted by Muslim extremists as part of their violent campaign against the West and their own governments. Jihad as a centerpiece of radical thought is illustrated by examining the doctrines of prominent extremist groups such as Hamas and Egyptian Islamic Jihad. Misuse of the term by prominent extremist leaders, such as by Osama bin Laden and others in the quote above, is also addressed.

THE CLASSICAL CONCEPT OF JIHAD

Qur'anic and Early Legal Perspectives

Muslims themselves have disagreed throughout their history about the meaning of the term jihad. In the Qur'an (or Koran), it is normally found in the sense of fighting in the path of God; this was used to describe warfare against the enemies of the early Muslim community (*ummah*). In the *hadith*, the second-most authoritative source of the *shari'a* (Islamic law), jihad is used to mean armed action, and most Islamic theologians and jurists in the classical period (the first three centuries) of Muslim history understood this obligation to be in a military sense.[1]

Islamic jurists saw jihad in the context of conflict in a world divided between the *Dar al-Islam* (territory under Islamic control) and the *Dar al-harb* (territory of war, which consisted of all lands not under Muslim rule). The inhabitants of the territory of war are divided between "People of the Book" (mainly Jews and Christians) and polytheists. This requirement to continue jihad until all of the world is included in the territory of Islam does not imply that Muslims must wage nonstop warfare, however. Although there was no mechanism for recognizing a non-Muslim government as legitimate, jurists allowed for the negotiation of truces and peace treaties of limited duration. Additionally, extending the territory of Islam does not mean the annihilation of all non-Muslims, nor even their necessary conversion: jihad cannot imply conversion by force, since the Qur'an (2:256) states that "There is no compulsion in religion." More than a religious aim, jihad really had a political one: the drive to establish a single, unified Muslim realm justified Islam's supercession of other faiths and allowed for the creation of a just political and social order.[2]

Jihad was generally understood not as an obligation of each individual Muslim (known as *fard 'ayn*) but as a general requirement of the Muslim community (*fard kifaya*). Only in emergencies, when the Dar al-Islam comes under unexpected attack, do all Muslims have to participate in jihad. Under normal circumstances, therefore, an individual Muslim need not take part so long as other Muslims carry the burden for all of defending the realm.[3]

Other Philosophical Perspectives

This consensus view of a restricted, defensive version of jihad was contested by Muslim legal philosopher Taqi al-Din Ahmad Ibn Taymiyya (1263–1328). He declared that a ruler who fails to enforce the shari'a rigorously in all aspects, including the conduct of jihad (and is therefore insufficiently Muslim), forfeits his right to rule. Ibn Taymiyya strongly advocated jihad as warfare against both the Crusaders and Mongols who then occupied parts of the Dar al-Islam, and most important, broke with the mainstream of Islam by asserting that a professing Muslim who does not live by the faith is an apostate (unbeliever). By going well beyond most jurists (who tolerated rulers who violated the shari'a for the sake of community stability), Ibn Taymiyya laid much of the groundwork for the intellectual arguments of contemporary radical Islamists.[4]

Islamic law condemns all warfare that does not qualify as jihad, specifically any warfare among Muslims. Thus, military action against Muslims is justified only by denying them the status of Muslims (e.g., classifying them as apostates or rebels).[5] Islamic juristic tradition is also very hostile toward terror as a means of political resistance. Classical Muslim jurists were remarkably tolerant toward political rebels by holding that they may not be executed nor their property confiscated. This tolerance vanished, however, for rebels who conducted attacks against unsuspecting and defenseless victims or who spread terror through abductions, rapes, the use of poisoned arrows and poisoning of wells (the chemical warfare of this period), arson, attacks against travelers, and night attacks. In these cases, jurists demanded harsh penalties (including death) and ruled that the punishment was the same whether the perpetrator or victim was Muslim or non-Muslim.[6]

Three main views of jihad thus coexisted in pre-modern times. In addition to the classical legal view of jihad as a compulsory, communal effort to defend and expand the Dar al-Islam, and Ibn Taymiyya's notion of active jihad as an indispensable feature of legitimate rule, there was also the *Sufi* movement's doctrine of *greater jihad*. The *Sufis* (a mystical sect of Islam) understood the greater jihad as an inner struggle against the base instincts of the body but also against corruption of the soul, and believed that the greater jihad is a necessary part of the process of gaining spiritual insight. To this day, most Muslims see jihad as a personal rather than a political struggle, while physical actions taken in defense of the realm are considered the *lesser jihad*. It is not surprising, then, that disagreement over the meaning of jihad has continued into the modern era.[7]

ORIGINS OF RADICAL IDEOLOGIES

Muslim reform movements in the Middle East first acquired a sense of urgency with the arrival of European imperialism in the latter part of the 19th century. The end of colonialism and acquisition of independence by most Muslim countries after World War II accelerated this drive.

However, the massive social changes that accompanied these reforms and the simultaneous introduction of new ideas that were alien to classical Islamic tradition—such as nationalism, popular sovereignty, and women's rights—disrupted traditional ways of life and caused traumatic dislocations in these societies.[8]

Disillusionment with the path Muslim societies have taken in the modern period reached its height in the 1970s. Increasingly widespread rejection of Western civilization as a model for Muslims to emulate has been accompanied by a search for indigenous values that reflect traditional Muslim culture, as well as a drive to restore power and dignity to the community. The last 30 years have seen the rise of militant, religiously-based political groups whose ideology focuses on demands for jihad (and the willingness to sacrifice one's life) for the forceful creation of a society governed solely by the shari'a and a unified Islamic state, and to eliminate un-Islamic and unjust rulers. These groups are also reemphasizing individual conformity to the requirements of Islam.[9]

Militant Islam (also referred to as political or radical Islam) is rooted in a contemporary religious resurgence in private and public life.[10] The causes of Islamic radicalism have been religio-cultural, political, and socio-economic and have focused on issues of politics and social justice such as authoritarianism, lack of social services, and corruption, which all intertwine as catalysts. Many Islamic reform groups have blamed social ills on outside influences; for example, modernization (e.g., Westernization and secularization) has been perceived as a form of neocolonialism, an evil that replaces Muslim religious and cultural identity and values with alien ideas and models of development.[11]

Islamic militancy is still not well understood by Americans. This is partly due to the secrecy which radical Islamic groups practice to protect themselves from the authorities and from outsiders who do not share their views and aims, but also because Western public communications media frequently tend to marginalize such groups. They are dismissed as religious fanatics, anti-Western hooligans, or mindless terrorists, without making an attempt to comprehend the deep discontents that have produced these Islamic groups' violent actions or the logic of their radical cause which compels them to behave as they do.[12]

DIFFERENCES IN SUNNI AND SHI'A INTERPRETATIONS OF JIHAD

Sunni and Shi'a (Shi'ite) Muslims agree, in terms of just cause, that jihad applies to the defense of territory, life, faith, and property; it is justified to repel invasion or its threat; it is necessary to guarantee freedom for the spread of Islam; and that difference in religion alone is not a sufficient cause. Some Islamic scholars have differentiated disbelief from persecution and injustice, and claimed that jihad is justified only to fight those unbelievers who have initiated aggression against the Muslim community. Others, however, have stated more militant views which were inspired by Islamic resistance to the European powers during the colonial period: in this view, jihad as "aggressive war" is authorized against all non-Muslims, whether they are oppressing Muslims or not.

The question of right authority—no jihad can be waged unless it is directed by a legitimate ruler—also has been divisive among Muslims. The Sunnis saw all of the Muslim caliphs (particularly the first four "rightly guided" caliphs to rule after the Prophet Muhammad's death, who possessed combined religious and political authority) as legitimate callers of jihad, as long as they had the support of the realm's *ulama* (Islamic scholars). The Shi'a see this power as having been meant for the Imams, but it was wrongly denied to them by the majority Sunnis. The lack of proper authority after the disappearance of the 12th ("Hidden") Imam in 874 A.D. also posed problems for the Shi'a; this was resolved by the ulama increasingly taking this authority for itself to the point where all legitimate forms of jihad may be considered defensive, and there is no restriction on the kind of war which may be waged in the Hidden Imam's absence so long as it is authorized by a just ruler (this idea reached its zenith under Iran's Ayatollah Ruhollah Khomeini).

Both sects agree on the other prerequisites for jihad. Right intention (*niyyah*) is fundamentally important for engaging in jihad. Fighting for the sake of conquest, booty, or honor in the eyes of one's companions will earn no reward; the only valid purpose for jihad is to draw near to God. In terms of last resort, jihad may be waged only if the enemy has first been offered the triple alternative: accept Islam, pay the *jizyah* (the poll tax required for non-Muslim "People of the Book" living under Muslim control), or fight.[13]

Conditions also are placed on the behavior of combatants in jihad: discrimination of noncombatants from warriors is required, along with the prohibition of harm to noncombatants such as women, children, the disabled, monks and rabbis (unless they are involved in the fighting), and those who have been given the promise of immunity; and proportionality, meaning that the least amount of force is used to obtain the desired ends in combat.[14]

IDEAS ON JIHAD IN THE MODERN ERA

Sayyid Abu al-A'la Mawdudi (1903–1979) was the first Islamist writer to approach jihad systematically. Warfare, in his view, is conducted not just to expand Islamic political dominance, but also to establish just rule (one that includes freedom of religion). For Mawdudi (an Indo-Pakistani who agitated for Pakistan's independence from India), jihad was akin to war of liberation, and is designed to establish politically independent Muslim states. Mawdudi's view significantly changed the concept of jihad in Islam and began its association with anticolonialism and "national liberation movements." His approach paved the way for Arab resistance to Zionism and the existence of the state of Israel to be referred to as jihad.[15]

Radical Egyptian Islamist thinkers (and members of the Muslim Brotherhood) Hasan al-Banna (1906–1949) and Sayyid Qutb (1906–1966) took hold of Mawdudi's activist and nationalist conception of jihad and its role in establishing a truly Islamic government, and incorporated Ibn Taymiyya's earlier conception of jihad that includes the overthrow of governments that fail to enforce the shari'a. This idea of revolution focuses first on dealing with the radicals' own un-Islamic rulers (the "near enemy") before Muslims can direct jihad against external enemies. If leaders such as Egyptian President Anwar Sadat, for example, are not true Muslims, then they cannot lead jihad, not even against a legitimate target such as Israel. Significantly, radical Islamists consider jihad mandatory for all Muslims, making it an individual rather than a communal duty.[16]

THE USE OF JIHAD BY ISLAMIC MILITANTS

Regional Islamic Militant Groups' Perceptions

Classical Islamic criteria for jihad were based on the early unified Muslim empire. The imposition of the modern nation-state on Middle East societies, however, has made such ideas no longer applicable; this can be seen by examining contemporary Muslim militant groups' ideologies.

The Islamic Resistance Movement (commonly known as Hamas) sees its situation as similar to that of the Muslim ruler Saladin in his struggle against the Christian Crusaders, as can be seen by examining portions of its Charter. The goal of Hamas is to establish an Islamic Palestinian state in place of Israel, through both violent means (including terrorism) and peaceful political activity. Hamas argues that the current situation of the Palestinians, living under Israeli control or dispersed from their homeland, is part of an ongoing crusade by Christians to take the Holy Lands out of Palestinian hands. The loss of Palestine and the creation of Israel, the

Charter continues, were brought about by the great powers of East and West, and taken together constitute a great tragedy not only for the Palestinians but for the entire Islamic community. This, Hamas proclaims, requires jihad not in the sense of expanding the territory of Islam, but of restoring it, and to recover land rather than conquer it. Nor is it a rebellion in the classical sense; rather, this is a struggle to regain a lost portion of the territory of Islam. The Hamas Charter thus provides a uniquely Islamic rationale for *al-intifada,* the "shaking off" of illegitimate rule.[17] This language thus seems to suggest defensive jihad, rather than an offensive struggle.

Since Hamas is not acting on behalf of an established government, it must find authorization elsewhere for its struggle against not only external enemies but also so-called "Muslim" governments that collaborate with the non-Muslim powers (by cooperating with Israel or allowing the basing of Western troops on their soil). The group considers Muslim governments that cooperate with the West as ignorant of the non-Muslim nations' true intentions, or corrupt. Hamas argues that it obtains its authority to declare jihad in another way: the Western powers' invasion of Islamic territory has created an emergency situation where Muslims cannot wait for authorization other than that given directly by God, so jihad is a required duty for all conscientious Muslims.[18] This exceptional situation suspends the usual lines between parties in a relationship so that every Muslim can participate in the struggle. Hamas' Charter thus relates the current situation of Muslims to the classical period, but also marks a break with that classical past. This extraordinary situation also means a change in the nature of Muslim obligation under jihad, from a collective responsibility to extend the Dar al-Islam to a duty for each individual Muslim to restore that territory.[19]

The same pattern of thinking is present in "The Neglected Duty," a pamphlet produced by Egyptian Islamic Jihad (or EIJ, the group that assassinated Anwar Sadat in 1981). This pamphlet, the group's announced "testament," is also a clear expression of the Sunni Islamist perspective on political violence as jihad. It argues that jihad as armed action is the heart of Islam, and that the neglect of this type of action by Muslims has caused the current depressed condition of Islam in the world. EIJ attempts to communicate a sense of urgency to Muslims, who are being victimized and whose territory is being divided and controlled by non-Muslim powers. The document also seeks to justify jihad against other Muslims who, because they are ignorant of this situation, actively cooperate with the unbelievers in the name of "modernization," and are worse than rebels—they are Muslim traitors and apostates. Furthermore, fighting such unbelievers without the limits imposed if they were rebellious Muslims is justified, since they are worse than other unbelievers.[20]

"The Neglected Duty" defines the current rulers of the Muslim world (as Sadat was defined) as the primary enemies of Islam and apostates, despite their profession of Islam and obedience to some of its laws, and advocates their execution. This document is explicitly messianic, asserting that Muslims must "exert every conceivable effort" to bring about the establishment of truly Islamic government, a restoration of the caliphate, and the expansion of the Dar al-Islam, and that the success of these endeavors is inevitable.[21] "The Neglected Duty" cites a different historical analogy for this struggle than does Hamas' Charter, however: more appropriate than the threat posed by the European Crusaders was the struggle of Muslims against the Mongol invaders.

EIJ is raising an important issue connected with irregular war: the group is advocating mass resistance against an established government, and such revolution can be justified in Islam only where the ruler becomes an unbeliever through public displays of unbelief. The most significant of such acts is introduction of an innovation (*bid'ah*), which is a policy, teaching, or action that violates precedents in the Qur'an or hadith. The leadership thus loses its divinely given authority when it commits apostasy, and Muslims not only must no longer obey such a ruler, but are required to revolt and depose him.

This reference to the obligation to God for the creation and maintenance of an Islamic state and the responsibilities of Muslims serves to answer the question of authorization for militant Islamic forces.[22] "The Neglected Duty" provides further justification for armed action by arguing that Egypt, like most of its neighbors, is not an Islamic state because its constitution and laws are a mix of traditional Islamic judgments and European law codes. Imposition of such a mixed legal system (non-Islamic laws that are an "innovation") by Egypt's leaders on their subjects thus means that the nation is not part of the territory of Islam, but part of the territory of war or unbelief.[23]

Shi'a radicals have a similar perspective to their Sunni extremist "brothers in arms." Ayatollah Ruhollah Khomeini (1902–1989) contended that Islamic jurists, "by means of jihad and enjoining the good and forbidding the evil, must expose and overthrow tyrannical rulers and rouse the people so the universal movement of all alert Muslims can establish Islamic government in the place of tyrannical regimes." The proper teaching of Islam will cause "the entire population to become *mujahids* [literally "strugglers for God]." Ayatollah Murtaza Mutahhari (1920–1979), a top ideologue of the Iranian Revolution, considered jihad a necessary consequence of Islam's content: by having political aims, Islam must sanction armed force and provide laws for its use. Mutahhari deemed jihad to be defensive, but his definition includes defense against oppression and may require what international law would consider a war of aggression. For example, he endorses an attack on a country of polytheists (some Muslims see Christians as polytheists due to Christianity's belief in a God who can exist in three manifestations) with the goal simply to eliminate polytheism's evils, not to impose Islam.[24]

Another radical Shi'a perspective on the justification for jihad can be found in the words of Shaykh Muhammad Hussein Fadlallah, spiritual leader of Lebanese Hizballah. In a 1986 interview, he stated that although violence is justified only for defensive purposes and as a last resort, the contemporary situation of the people of the Middle East, in particular of Muslims, creates a scenario that breeds violence. The establishment of Israel, the dislocation of the Palestinians, and the interference of a great oppressive power (in other words, the United States) in Arab–Islamic political, economic, and social affairs leads some Muslims (e.g., militant groups) to consider themselves justified in using force to achieve their goals, and this can even sometimes lead to extreme behavior.[25] Fadlallah does clarify that terrorism (*hudna,* or violence in Arabic) is not legitimate or justified in Islam, to include the destruction of life, kidnapping, or the hijacking of airliners or ships, and suggests that militants have gone too far in the conduct of their struggle when they employ such means. Nevertheless, he concludes by informing the American people that it is up to them to improve the situation by pressing for reforms in the policies of their government.[26]

How should the West respond to Islamic militant groups? Shaykh Fadlallah suggests that the West should listen to the anger expressed by such groups. While stressing that the way to peace is through dialogue, Fadlallah said that the West must first recognize that Muslims who act in ways that are harmful to Western interests are responding to pain of their own. Islam, he added, should not be thought of as uncompromisingly hostile to the West, since militant groups do not speak for all of the community. Fadlallah adds that if the West does listen to these groups, however, it will understand that the concerns these groups have (for justice, human rights, and self-determination) are legitimate, even if their methods are excessive.[27]

Al Qaeda and Transnational Jihad: A New Twist on Old Complaints

Before his emergence as the prime suspect in the 9/11 attacks, Osama bin Laden had described his goals and grievances and the tactics of his transnational at Qaeda network in great detail in a series of statements and interviews. Taken together, these statements provide insight into an ideology that may seem abhorrent or crazy to Americans but has been carefully crafted to appeal to the disgruntled and dispossessed of the Islamic world.[28] Bin Laden's ideology, however, is really more political than religious.

At the heart of bin Laden's philosophy are two declarations of war—jihad—against the United States. The first, his *Bayan* (statement) issued on 26 August 1996, was directed specifically at "Americans occupying the land of the two holy places," as bin Laden refers to the cities of Mecca and Medina that are located in his native Saudi Arabia. Here he calls upon Muslims all over the world to fight to "expel the infidels . . . from the Arab Peninsula."[29] In his fatwa of 23 February 1998, titled "Declaration of the World Islamic Front for Jihad Against the Jews and Crusaders," which he issued along with the leaders of extremist groups in Egypt, Pakistan, and Bangladesh, bin Laden broadened his earlier edict. In the fatwa, he specifies that the radicals' war is a defensive struggle against Americans and their allies who have declared war "on God, his Messenger, and Muslims." The "crimes and sins" perpetrated by the United States are threefold: first, it "stormed" the Arabian peninsula during the Gulf War and has continued "occupying the lands of Islam in the holiest of places"; second, it continues a war of annihilation against Iraq; and third, the United States supports the state of Israel and its continued occupation of Jerusalem. The only appropriate Muslim response, according to the fatwa, is a defensive jihad to repulse the aggressor; therefore, borrowing from classical and modern Islamic scholars (because it is defensive), such a war is a moral obligation incumbent upon all true Muslims.[30]

Bin Laden's anger at the "American crusader forces" who are "occupying" his homeland stems from an injunction from the Prophet that there "not be two religions in Arabia"; the presence of foreign forces on holy soil is thus an intolerable affront to 1,400 years of Islamic tradition. In his 1996 statement of jihad, bin Laden blamed the serious economic crisis then gripping Saudi Arabia (due to falling oil prices and widespread corruption) on the presence of these Western "crusader forces." Two years later, in his 1998 fatwa, bin Laden charged that the United States was not only occupying and plundering Arabia, but was "using its bases in the peninsula as a spearhead to fight against the neighboring Islamic peoples." In bin Laden's war, the goal of expelling the "Judeo-Christian enemy" from Islamic holy lands should occur first on the Arabian peninsula, then in Iraq (which for 500 years was the seat of the Islamic caliphate), and third in Palestine, site of the Al-Aqsa Mosque in Jerusalem (which is sacred to Muslims as the place from where Muhammad ascended to heaven).[31]

Although the initial attacks associated with bin Laden occurred in Saudi Arabia, Somalia, East Africa, and Yemen, he increasingly made clear that he would bring the war to the American homeland. Al Qaeda is believed to have aided the first attack against the World Trade Center in 1993, and bin Laden told an ABC News reporter in May 1998 that the battle will "inevitably move . . . to American soil."[32] Although he appears to be fired by the religious zeal of Saudi Arabia's puritanical Wahhabi movement, bin Laden's targets have not been offending religious and cultural institutions, but political, military, and economic targets. Additionally, though he quotes selective (but incomplete) passages from the Qur'an to establish the basis for the jihad, bin Laden's motivations are really not that different from the anti-imperialistic doctrines that sustain religious and nonreligious extremist groups all over the world.[33]

In return for joining the jihad against America, bin Laden has promised his followers an honored place in paradise, in accordance with a statement in the Qur'an that "a martyr's privileges are guaranteed by Allah." Bin Laden and many of the other Islamic militant groups in the Middle East are able to draw on large numbers of enthusiastic and waiting recruits for their war against the United States—impoverished youths who are ready to die simply for the idea of jihad.

"Jihad Factories": An Enduring Legacy of Hatred

It is estimated that more than one million young men from Pakistan, Afghanistan, Central Asia, and the Muslim parts of China are attending *madrassas,* or private Islamic religious schools, every year in Pakistan. Madrassa students spend most of their day in rote memorization of the Qur'an in Arabic (this is not their native language, so few understand what they are reading) and interpreting the hadith. Only theology is taught; there is no math, science, computer training, or secular history.[34] The young men at these schools are drawn from the dire poor of the societies they come from, kept in self-contained worlds that are isolated from outside influences, and indoctrinated with a powerful, not-so-academic radical message: their highest honor and duty is to wage jihad to defend Islam from its attackers, and the United States is the chief enemy of Islam.[35]

Madrassas, which have a tradition in Pakistan that dates from colonial days of promoting political independence along with their religious teaching, fill a significant gap in the underfunded public school system by offering free tuition, room, and board. Madrassas received state funding during the Afghan War when they were used to groom the mujahedin who were being sent to fight the Soviet invaders.[36] Many of these schools were emptied in the 1990s when the Taliban needed assistance in military campaigns against its Northern Alliance foes, and many students sent to the front did not return. The graduates of these madrassas have also turned up in places like Bosnia, Chechnya, and the Kashmir, and the survivors of those conflicts have taken their battlefield experience back to their home countries where it is being put to use in jihads against their own not-Islamic-enough governments and societies.

The readiness of millions of young men trained in these schools to sacrifice their lives for Islam—and their unquestioning acceptance of anti-American and pro-Islamic extremist propaganda—will continue to be a powerful and enduring weapon against the US-led global war on terrorism, and one that bin Laden and other militants who are bent on attacking the United States and its allies can call on in the years ahead.

ACCEPTANCE OF MILITANTS' IDEAS AND METHODS IS LIMITED

The thrust of the entire jihad tradition which Islamic radicals have "hijacked" makes it clear that not everything is permissible. Although the language in the Qur'an and hadith and in other classical Muslim sources is overwhelmingly militant in many places, this is a reflection of the Muslims' world in the seventh century, which consisted initially of resistance to a variety of more powerful non-Islamic tribes and then successful military campaigns to spread the faith. Besides containing exhortations to fight, however, Islamic sacred texts have also laid out the rules of engagement for war, which (as mentioned earlier) included prohibitions against the killing of noncombatants such as women, children, the aged, and disabled. These texts also require notice to the adversary before an attack, require that a Muslim army must seek peace if its opponent does, and forbid committing aggression against others and suicide.[37] Those who are unfamiliar with the Qur'an and hadith can miss these points when confronted with the propagandistic calls to jihad of militant Islamic groups.

The actions of rebels in the classical period of Islam encountered widespread resentment and condemnation, and this strong sentiment against rebellion remains in modern Islamic thought. Most Muslims agree with the presumption in Islamic teachings on war that individuals are innocent and therefore not subject to harm unless they demonstrate by their actions that they are a threat to the safety or survival of Muslims. On this basis, the overwhelming majority of Islamic scholars have for centuries rejected indiscriminate killing and the terrorizing of civilian populations as a legitimate form of jihad.[38] Also, at no point do Islamic sacred texts even consider the horrific and random slaughter of uninvolved bystanders that is represented by the 9/11 airliner attacks; most Muslims throughout the world were as shocked by those attacks as Americans were.

The radical message in works such as Hamas' Charter, "The Neglected Duty," and the writings of Khomeini and his fellow revolutionary Iranian Shi'a clerics nevertheless finds a lot of acceptance with contemporary Muslims. The reason is simply because of the poor socioeconomic circumstances and lack of human dignity that many Muslim peoples find themselves subject to, brought about by secular failures to attend to their problems.[39] Militant Islamic groups, exemplified by Hamas and the Palestinian branch of Islamic Jihad, have been able to use such poor conditions to their advantage. They provide social services (such as operating free or low-cost schools, medical clinics, sports clubs, and women's support groups), many of which the Palestinian Authority itself often cannot provide, to build public support and attract recruits in the occupied territories.[40]

Public statements over the last several months by some moderate Muslim religious authorities and commentators that Islamic extremists are corrupting a peaceful religious faith for their own twisted ends are encouraging. Equally positive is the growing recognition in the Muslim world both of bin Laden's lack of proper religious qualifications to issue any religious edicts that promote jihad, and his lack of success, on a strategic level, in forcing the United States to withdraw its military forces completely from Saudi Arabia or to give up its campaign against Islamic terrorism. A few prominent Muslim scholars have not only condemned the terrorist attacks upon the United States, but have declared the perpetrators of these attacks to be "suicides," not martyrs. This is significant, since Islam forbids

suicide and teaches that its practitioners are sent not to paradise but to hell, where they are condemned to keep repeating their suicidal act for eternity.[41]

CONCLUSION

As described herein, jihad in Islamic thought and practice possesses a range of meanings, with Muslim radicals focusing on the physical, violent form of struggle to resist what they see as cultural, economic, military, and political assaults from outside the ummah and oppression and injustice within. So long as societal conditions within many Muslim states remain poor, with unrepresentative governments (which are seen to be propped up by the United States) that are unwilling or unable to undertake meaningful but difficult reforms, then militant Islamic groups will continue to attract recruits and financial support. In spite of logical fallacies and inconsistencies in the doctrine of jihad of radical Islamic groups, and the fact that most of the broad constituency they are attempting to appeal to does not buy into their ideology or methods, such groups nevertheless remain as significant threats to US interests everywhere in the world.

The challenge for the US government over the next several years will be to encourage and support lasting reform by Muslim states who are our allies in the Middle East, while maintaining a more balanced and fair-minded foreign policy toward all key regional players. We must also do a better job of countering the Islamic extremists' widely disseminated version of jihad, while being more persuasive that our own government—and our society—are truly not anti-Islamic. Such actions will do much to deny a supportive environment to our radical Muslim foes. For its part, the US military needs to better understand the religious and cultural aspects of our adversaries' asymmetric mindset—in this case, how Islamic militants conceive of and use jihad—to be successful and survivable in its global campaign against terrorism.

Notes

1. Bernard Lewis, *The Political Language of Islam* (Chicago: Univ. of Chicago Press, 1988), p. 72, as quoted in Douglas E. Streusand, "What Does Jihad Mean?" *Middle East Quarterly*, 4 (September 1997), 1.
2. Streusand, p. 2.
3. Ibid.
4. Emmanuel Sivan, *Radical Islam: Medieval Theology and Modern Politics* (New Haven: Yale Univ. Press, 1990), p. 101; as quoted in Streusand, pp. 2–3.
5. Fred M. Donner, "The Sources of Islamic Conceptions of War," in *Just War and Jihad: Historical and Theoretical Perspectives on War and Peace in Western and Islamic Traditions*, ed. John Kelsay and James Turner Johnson (New York: Greenwood Press, 1991), pp. 51–52, as quoted in Streusand, p. 3.
6. Khaled Abou El Fadl, "Terrorism Is at Odds with Islamic Tradition," *Los Angeles Times*, 22 August 2001.
7. Streusand, pp. 3–4.
8. Johannes J. G. Jansen, *The Neglected Duty: The Creed of Sadat's Assassins and Islamic Resurgence in the Middle East* (New York: Macmillan, 1986), pp. xi–xii.
9. Ibid., pp. xii–xiii.
10. The term "fundamentalism" is also used incorrectly in conjunction with Islam to describe this phenomenon, but this concept is really more appropriate to American Christian thought, whence it originated.
11. John L. Esposito, "Political Islam and the West," *Military Technology*, February 2001, pp. 89–90.
12. Jansen, pp. xiii–xiv.
13. Mehdi Abedi and Gary Legenhausen, eds., *Jihad and Shahadat: Struggle and Martyrdom in Islam* (Houston: Institute for Research and Islamic Studies, 1986), pp. 21–23.
14. Ibid., pp. 23–24.
15. Streusand, p. 5.
16. Sivan, pp. 16–21 and 114–16, as quoted in Streusand, p. 5.
17. John Kelsay, *Islam and War: A Study in Comparative Ethics* (Louisville, Ky.: Westminster/John Knox Press, 1993), pp. 95–97.
18. Kelsay bases his discussion on the translation by Muhammad Maqdsi, titled "Charter of the Islamic Resistance Movement (Hamas) of Palestine" (Dallas: Islamic Association for Palestine, 1990), pp. 17–18. Another translation of this document, by Raphael Israeli, is available on the Internet at www.ict.org.il/documents/documentdet.cfm? docid = 14.
19. Kelsay, *Islam and War*, p. 98.
20. Ibid., pp. 100–01.
21. Jansen, p. 162, as quoted in Streusand, p. 5.
22. Kelsay, *Islam and War*, pp. 101–02.
23. Ibid., p. 102.
24. Abedi and Legenhausen, p. 89, as quoted in Streusand, p. 6.
25. Kelsay, *Islam and War*, p. 109.
26. Ibid., pp. 109–10.
27. Quoted in Kelsay, *Islam and War*, p. 108.
28. Michael Dobbs, "Inside the Mind of Osama Bin Laden," *The Washington Post*, 20 September 2001.
29. Ibid.
30. Sohail Hashmi, "The Terrorists' Zealotry Is Political Not Religious," *The Washington Post*, 30 September 2001. For a good analysis of Bin Laden's fatwa, including its historical background, see Bernard Lewis, "License to Kill," *Foreign Affairs*, 77 (November/December 1998), 14–19. The translated text of the fatwa itself is available on the Federation of American Scientists' website at www.fas.org/irp/world/para/docs/980223-fatwa.htm.
31. Dobbs.
32. Ibid.
33. Hashmi.
34. Jeffrey Goldberg, "Inside Jihad U.: The Education of a Holy Warrior," *New York Times Magazine*, 25 July 2000.
35. Indira A. R. Lakshmanan, "In Some Schools, Jihad, Anger at US Are Lessons," *Boston Globe*, 4 October 2001.
36. Ibid.
37. Teresa Watanabe, "Extremists Put Own Twist on Islamic Faith," *Los Angeles Times*, 24 September 2001.
38. Hashmi.
39. Jansen, p. 2.
40. "Islamic Groups Going for Goodwill," *Daily Progress* (Charlottesville, Va.), 18 November 1998, p. A8.
41. Bernard Lewis, "Jihad vs. Crusade," *The Wall Street Journal*, 27 September 2001.

Discussion Questions

1. What was the classical concept of jihad according to Knapp?
2. What was Ibn Taymiyya's view of jihad? By contrast, describe the Sufi doctrine of greater jihad.
3. How does Knapp explain the origin of militant or radical Islam?
4. What are the prerequisites for jihad in the view of both Sunni and Shi'a Muslims? How do the two sects disagree?
5. According to Knapp, how did the idea of jihad change in the modern era?
6. How do militant Islamic groups such as Hamas or Egyptian Islamic Jihad use the concept of jihad?
7. What are the radical Shi'a perspectives on jihad?
8. Explains Osama bin Laden's ideology.

Discussion Questions

1. Compare the classical doctrine of jihad with the just war theory. How are they different? How are they similar?
2. Knapp says that Islam is a religion of peace that has been hijacked by radicals. Do you agree? Why or why not?
3. How should the United States and allies deal with Osama bin Laden and other radicals? Explain your view.

Problem Cases

1. The Iraq War

After a long buildup, U.S. and British troops invaded Iraq in March 2003. Only two months later, in May 2003, President Bush declared combat operations over. But the fighting continued, and in April 2004, the war began again in Fallujah, a Sunni town that had been a center of anti-Americanism. The Sunni Muslim insurgents fired rocket-propelled grenades and Kalashnikovs at American troops. More than 1,300 U.S. troops responded with attack helicopters, tanks, and warplanes. In the first two weeks of April, more than 80 American soldiers and 900 Iraqi were killed, and 561 U.S. troops were wounded. Hospital workers claimed that the Iraqi dead were mostly women, children, and elderly. By the beginning of June 2004 the total number of American casualties was 812 dead and 4,637 wounded, according to the official count released by the U.S. military. Other estimates were 7,000 to 10,000 U.S. soldiers treated for illness or injury, including noncombat injury. The Iraqi casualties including civilians were estimated to be about 10,000. The total U.S. cost for the war was over a billion dollars and counting. (The source for these numbers was http://www.antiwar.com/casualties.)

What was the justification for this war? First, there was the prevention argument. In its most basic form, this is the argument that if one nation threatens another, then the threatened nation is justified in attacking the nation making the threat. The Bush administration perceived Iraq to be a potential threat to the United States and her allies, and that was the reason given for attacking. In the words of President Bush's National Security Statement (National Security of the United States of America (2002) http://www.whitehouse.gov/nsc/nss9.html), the United States must "stop rogue states and their terrorist clients before they are able to threaten or use weapons of mass destruction against the United States and our allies and friends." The problem with this statement is that Iraq did not have the alleged weapons of mass destruction or programs to develop them. According to Hans Blix, the head of the UN inspections team, the UN inspections had been effective in eliminating the weapons or programs to develop them. (See his book *Disarming Iraq* in the Suggested Readings.) Investigations by members of Congress and others revealed that the Bush administration had no solid evidence of the existence of the weapons or programs. The so-called evidence for the weapons or weapons programs, including Colin Powell's speech to the UN, can be found on the CIA website (http://www.cia.org) in the special section on the War on Terrorism. Richard A. Clark, the counterterrorism czar in both the Clinton and Bush administrations, claimed that President Bush was eager to attack Iraq from the beginning of his administration, and after the 9/11 attacks he tried to link Saddam Hussein and al Qaeda despite the lack of evidence. (See his book *Against All Enemies* in the Suggested Readings.)

But for the sake of discussion, let's assume that Iraq had the weapons of mass destruction in 2003. Would this have justified the invasion and occupation of Iraq? Perhaps, but we have to assume that Saddam Hussein would have handed these weapons over to terrorists, and risk serious reprisal. It is hard to see how that would have been in his self-interest. His reason for developing these weapons, it could be argued, was that he wanted them for self-defense. North Korea was named by President Bush as one of the nations making up the axis of evil (along with Iran and Iraq), but North Korea was not attacked by the United States because North Korea had nuclear weapons. It is not hard to see why North Korea, Iran, India, Pakistan, Israel, France, Germany, Russia, and other nations want these weapons.

The general problem with the prevention argument is that it makes it too easy to justify war. War should be the last resort, not the first thing considered. Even Henry Kissinger, surely no peacenik, acknowledged this problem when he warned against using the appeal to prevention as a universal principle available to every nation. (See Henry Kissinger, "Our Intervention in Iraq," *Washington Post* op-ed, August 12, 2002.) For example, during the cold war, the USSR was certainly threatened by the United States, which had thousands of missiles with nuclear warheads targeting Russian cities and military bases. Did this threat justify a Russian first strike? North Korea is a rogue state that actually has nuclear weapons, and may be selling them to other countries. Are we justified in attacking North Korea? Why not attack Iran, the other country in the axis of evil? For that matter, isn't Saudi Arabia a threat, since it is the country that encouraged the fundamentalist and militant religion that produced Osama bin Laden and his terrorist organization?

Second, the war was justified by the humanitarian argument that Saddam Hussein was a brutal dictator, comparable to Hitler no less, and needed to be removed from power. No doubt Saddam was an evil man, having launched aggressive wars against Iran and Kuwait, gassed thousands of Kurds, killed numerous rivals, and at least attempted to develop chemical, biological, and nuclear weapons before this was stopped by the UN inspections. But this seems to be an argument for assassination, not war. The CIA has tried to kill Fidel Castro several times because he was perceived to be evil, but the United States has not launched a massive invasion of Cuba. Why not? (The Bay of Pigs operation was not exactly an all-out military campaign like the Iraq War.) Furthermore, like the prevention argument, the humanitarian argument makes it too easy to justify war. Should we go to war against any and all counties ruled by evil men (or women)?

Third, there was the legalistic argument that war with Iraq was necessary to enforce United Nations resolutions in the face of Iraqi defiance. But France, Germany, and other member nations of the UN argued that more inspections would do the job, since Iraq was allowing them. And in the event that war was necessary, it should have been undertaken by a coalition of the member nations, and not just by the United States and Britain (although a few other nations contributed token forces.)

As the bloody occupation continued on in 2004, pundits, analysts, and journalists offered various other justifications for the war and occupation. One was the nation-building argument, the view that turning the despotic regimes in the Middle East into democracies like the United States would be a good thing. This view was attributed to Bush administration officials such as Paul Wolfowitz. But if this is such a good idea, then it would apply to nations such as Saudi Arabia, which is no democracy. Another was that the war was really an extension of the fight against al Qaeda. This justification assumed that there were close ties between al Qaeda operatives and Saddam Hussein, even though there was no evidence of this. Against this, there was the claim that the Muslim terrorists hated the secular government of Saddam Hussein. Critics of the war maintained that the real reason for the war was President Bush getting back at his father's enemy. European critics thought the war was really about oil—Americans wanted to control one of the world's largest oil reserves. They pointed to the fact that Haliburton, the company run by Dick Cheney before he became Vice President, was immediately given the contract to re-build Iraq's oil industry.

All things considered, was the Iraq war justified or not? Can you justify it using just war theory? Can you justify it some other way? Explain your view.

2. Torture at Abu Ghraib

(Reported by Seymour M. Hersh in *The New Yorker,* May 10, 17, and 24, 2004. Also see Susan Sontag, "Regarding The Torture Of Others," *The New York Times Magazine,* May 23, 2004).

The 1984 Convention Against Torture and Other Cruel, Inhuman or Degrading Treatment or Punishment defines torture as "any act by which severe pain or suffering, whether physical or mental, is intentionally inflicted on a person for such purposes as obtaining from him or a third person information or a confession." (Quoted by Sontag, p. 25) The federal criminal statute that implements the convention (Title 18, section 2340, available online at www4.law.cornell.edu/uscode/18/2340.html) defines torture as an act "intended to inflict severe physical or mental pain or suffering upon another person." Included is the threat of imminent death or the threat of severe physical pain or suffering.

By this definition, many prisoners at the Abu Ghraib prison in Iraq were tortured. There is the well-known picture of the hooded man forced to stand on a box with wires attached to his hands and neck. Reportedly he was told that he would be electrocuted if he stepped or fell off the box. Former prisoners tell stories of U.S. soldiers beating prisoners, sometimes to death. Mohammed Unis Hassan says that he was cuffed to the bars of his cell and then a female soldier poked his eye with her fingers so hard he couldn't see afterward. Now his left eye is gray and glassy and his vision is blurred. He says he saw an old man forced to lie naked on his face until he died. Other naked prisoners were threatened and bitten by attack dogs.

Some of the mistreatment involved sexual humiliation. There are photographs of naked Iraqi prisoners forced to simulate oral or anal sex. Private Lynndie England is shown giving a thumbs-up sign and pointing at the genitals of a naked and hooded Iraqi as he masturbates. In another picture, Private England is shown with Specialist Charles A. Graner; both are grinning and giving the thumbs-up sign in front of a pile of naked Iraqis, piled on top of each other in a pyramid. Another picture shows Private England leading a naked man around on a dog leash.

Many people think this humiliating treatment of the Iraqi prisoners is indefensible. But not everyone agrees. On his radio show Rush Limbaugh claimed that the humiliation was just harmless fun, similar to what goes on in college fraternities or secret societies. He said, "This is no different than what happens at the Skull and Bones initiation, and we're going to ruin people's lives over it. . . because they had a good time." (Quoted by Sontag, pp. 28–29) Certainly Private England and Specialist Graner appear to be having a good time.

One way of defending some of the mistreatment, then, is to deny that sexual humiliation is torture. Torture involves extreme physical pain. One thinks of medieval tortures such as the rack, the thumbscrew, or branding irons. But sexual humiliation doesn't involve extreme physical pain. It is just embarrassing or humiliating, like the sort of things that go on in fraternity initiation rites.

An objection to this view is that homosexual acts and public nakedness are not harmless fun in the culture and religion of Islam, but serious violations. Otherwise it would not be humiliating and demeaning. Does this imply that the sexual humiliation of Iraqi prisoners amounts to torture? What is your position?

Secretary of Defense Donald Rumsfeld adopted a similar view of the mistreatment of prisoners. According to Seymour M. Hersh, Secretary Rumsfeld approved a secret operation called Copper Green, which encouraged the use of coercion and sexual humiliation to get information about the insurgents in Iraq. Apparently Secretary Rumsfeld made a distinction between torture and coercion or sexual humiliation. Torture is the infliction of severe physical pain, and as such it is wrong and illegal. But coercion or sexual humiliation is not torture because it does not involve severe physical pain. Examples of coercion include handcuffing with flexi-cuffs which cut off circulation and cause skin lesions, solitary confinement, sensory deprivation, hooding, sleep deprivation, withholding of food and water, constant loud noise, extremes of cold or hot, and so-called stress positions such as squatting or standing with the arms lifted. One technique used by the CIA on al Qaeda detainees is water boarding, in which a prisoner is strapped down on a board, then pushed under water. Sexual humiliation includes being paraded naked outside of other cells in front of other prisoners and guards, being handcuffed naked to the bars of a cell, being forced to masturbate or engage in sodomy, being pulled around on a dog leash while naked, being put in piles of naked bodies, and so on.

Is there a clear distinction between torture and coercion or sexual humiliation? Doesn't coercion or sexual humiliation produce extreme mental pain? Is coercion or sexual humiliation morally justified if it produces no useful information? What do you think?

Suppose we grant a distinction between torture, defined as acts causing severe pain and suffering, and torture lite, as I shall call it, which supposedly causes only moderate pain and suffering. Torture lite would include sexual humiliation and the techniques of coercion listed above. Is the torture lite of prisoners morally and legally allowed? Why or why not?

A different defense of torture used by the Bush administration is to hold that every captured prisoner is an enemy combatant or terrorist having no rights. This means that the Iraqis are not soldiers protected by the Geneva Conventions or federal laws that forbid torture. Torture of enemy combatants or terrorists is justified if it yields information valuable in the War Against Terrorism.

Is torture (whether real or lite) justified if it produces life-saving information? Suppose that one of the Abu Ghraib prisoners revealed information that enabled the U.S. forces to prevent a suicide bombing. Would this information justify the mistreatment of the prisoners at Abu Ghraib? Why or why not?

The best philosophical article on torture is Henry Shue's "Torture," *Philosophy and Public Affairs* 7, 2 (Winter 1978), pp. 124–43. Shue argues that torture is morally justified in some cases. The example he uses to support his case is very relevant in today's world. Suppose a terrorist has hidden a nuclear bomb in the heart of New York City. If it is not defused it will explode and kill millions of innocent people. Is it permissible to torture the terrorist to find out where the bomb is hidden so that it can be defused? Isn't this better than letting the bomb explode? Isn't this torture justified by the principle of proportionality? Why or why not?

3. Jose Padilla

Mr. Padilla, 31, was born in Brooklyn and raised in Chicago. He served prison time for a juvenile murder in Illinois and for gun possession in Florida. He converted to Islam in prison and took the name Abdullah al Muhijir when he lived in Egypt. According to the government, he also spent time in Saudi Arabia, Pakistan, and Afghanistan.

Mr. Padilla was taken into custody by the FBI in May 2002 when he arrived from overseas at Chicago's O'Hare International Airport. Then he was held incommunicado at a Navy brig in Charleston, S.C., where he was denied access to counsel. No formal charges were brought against Mr. Padilla, but not long after his arrest, Attorney General John Ashcroft claimed that Mr. Padilla was part of a plot by al Qaeda to explode a radiological "dirty bomb."

On December 18, 2003, a federal appeals court in Manhattan ruled (2–1) that the president does not have the executive authority to hold American citizens indefinitely without access to lawyers simply by declaring them "enemy combatants." The two-judge majority decision said that the president does not have the constitutional authority as commander in chief to detain as enemy combatants American citizens seized on American soil, away from the zone of combat. Furthermore, the ruling said, citing a 1971 statue, that the detention of an American citizen under the circumstances of Mr. Padilla's case was not authorized by Congress.

On the same day as the court's decision, the Department of Justice issued a statement on the case. (The statement can be found at http://www.ssdoj.gov., and there is a link to the text of the court's decision.) The government's statement said that Padilla was associated with senior al Qaeda leaders including Osama bin Laden and that he had received training from al Qaeda operatives on wiring explosive devices and on the construction of a uranium-enhanced explosive device. The statement concluded that Jose Padilla "is an enemy combatant who poses a serious and continuing threat to the American people and our national security."

The court ordered the government to release Mr. Padilla from military custody. But he could still face criminal charges or be detained as a material witness in connection with grand jury proceedings. Do you agree with the court's decision? Why or why not?

In addition to Mr. Padilla, some 600 men of varying nationalities are being held at the Guantanamo Bay naval base in Cuba. These men were captured in Afghanistan and Pakistan during the operations against the Taliban. Like Mr. Padilla they are deemed by the U.S. government to be "enemy combatants" having no legal rights. They are not being allowed to contest their detention through petitions for habeas corpus, the ancient writ which for centuries has been used in the English-speaking world to challenge the legality of confinement.

The basic issue is whether or not the president should have the power to deny basic rights in the name of fighting terrorism. What is your view of this?

4. Fighting Terrorism

What can the United States do to prevent terrorist attacks like the September 11 assault on the World Trade Center and the Pentagon? One proposal is national identity cards, discussed by Daniel J. Wakin in *The New York Times*, October 7, 2001. According to polls taken after the attacks, about 70 percent of Americans favor such cards, which are used in other countries. French citizens are required to carry national ID cards, and they may be stopped by the police for card inspection at any time. Such cards are also required in Belgium, Greece, Luxembourg, Portugal, and Spain. Privacy International, a watchdog group in London, estimates that about one hundred countries have compulsory national IDs. Some, like Denmark, issue ID numbers at birth, around which a lifetime of personal information accumulates.

It is not clear if required ID cards would violate the U.S. Constitution. One objection is that a police demand to see the card would constitute a "seizure" forbidden by the Fourth Amendment. Another objection is that illegal immigrants would be targeted rather than terrorists. But proponents of the cards argue that they could be used to identify terrorists and protect travelers. Larry Ellison, the chief executive of the software maker Oracle, claims that people's fingerprints could be embedded on the cards and police or airport guards could scan the cards and check the fingerprints against a database of terrorists. The cards could protect airline travelers at check-in and guard against identity theft. Advocates of the cards argue that there is already a great deal of personal information gathered by private industry, any invasion of privacy caused by the ID cards would not matter much. What do you think? Are national ID cards a good way to fight against terrorism?

Another proposal is to allow suspicionless searches. In Israel, the police can search citizens and their belongings at any time without any particular cause or suspicion. These searches are conducted at shopping centers, airports, stadiums, and other public places. Citizens are also required to pass through metal detectors before entering public places. The U.S. Constitution requires police to have an objective suspicion or "probable cause" to search you, your belongings, or your car, but the Supreme Court has granted exceptions such as border searches and drunk-driving checkpoints. Why not allow suspicionless searches at public places like shopping centers, airports, and football stadiums?

Even more controversial is racial profiling. Israeli authorities single out travelers and citizens for questioning and searches based on racial profiling. Experts cite vigorous racial profiling as one of the reasons Israeli airplanes are not hijacked. The U.S. Supreme Court has not ruled on whether racial profiling violates the equal protection clause of the U.S. Constitution and has declined to hear cases on the practice. Opinions differ on what counts as racial profiling and when or if it is unconstitutional. Advocates of the practice claim that police already practice racial profiling and that it is effective in preventing crime. Critics object that it is nothing more than racism. Is racial profiling justified in the fight against terrorism?

In Canada, police are allowed to arrest and hold suspected terrorists without charges and without bail for up to ninety days. In France, suspects can be held for questioning for nearly five days without being charged and without having any contact with an attorney. Britain's antiterrorist legislation allows suspicious individuals to be detained for up to seven days without a court appearance. The new antiterrorist legislation proposed by the U.S. Congress would allow authorities to hold foreigners suspected of terrorist activity for up to a week without charges. Is this indefinite holding without charges and without bail acceptable?

Finally, in the fight against terrorism Israel has condoned assassinations or "judicially sanctioned executions," that is, killing terrorist leaders such as Osama bin Laden. The United States does not currently permit assassination, but this prohibition stems from an executive order that could be repealed, not because it is forbidden by the Constitution. Should the United States reconsider its position on assassination?

In general, are these methods of fighting terrorism acceptable to you or not? Why or why not?

5. National Missile Defense

National Missile Defense (NMD) is the controversial $8.3-billion missile defense shield championed by President George W. Bush and his Secretary of Defense, Donald Rumsfeld. It is an updated version of President Reagan's Strategic Defense Initiative. More than $60 billion already has been spent on the missile defense program in the last two decades.

The basic idea of NMD is appealing. Instead of ensuring peace by relying on the Cold War strategy of MAD (mutual assured destruction), where neither the

United States nor Russia can defend against nuclear attack but can destroy the other if attacked, NMD would protect the United States from missile attack with a defensive umbrella of antimissile missiles. This would give the United States an advantage over Russia or other nuclear powers not having any missile defense.

Russia is no longer seen as the main threat, even though Russia still has thousands of long-range missiles left over from the Cold War arms race. According to President Bush, the main threat to the United States comes from so-called rogue nations unfriendly to the United States such as North Korea and Iraq. In view of the September 11 attacks, the al Qaeda terrorist network of Osama bin Laden also should be considered a threat. Bin Laden has promised more terrorist attacks on the United States and has proclaimed a jihad against the United States. Even though these terrorists do not possess nuclear weapons or missiles at present (or as far as we know, they don't) it seems likely that they will acquire them in the future. Then they could hold America hostage by threatening a nuclear attack or they might launch a surprise attack on an undefended American city such as New York City or Los Angeles.

Even though it seems like a good idea, NMD has problems. There is a good chance that it would not work in an actual attack. Two out of four major missile defense tests conducted so far have failed. Critics say that trying to hit a missile with another missile is like trying to shoot down a bullet with another bullet. It is difficult, to say the least. Countermeasures such as dummy missiles or balloons could fool the defense system. Low-tech missiles, the most likely to be used, do not go in a predictable path so they would be missed by antimissile missiles.

Even if the defensive system worked perfectly, it would only defend against long-range missiles and not against nuclear weapons delivered by other means. For example, a short-range missile could be launched from a submarine just off the coast, or a weapon could be taken to its target by truck or a private shipper. The most likely scenario is that terrorists would assemble a nuclear weapon at the target and then explode it. Obviously, NMD is no defense against such terrorist attacks.

Finally, there are political problems. NMD violates the 1972 Antiballistic Missile Treaty with Russia. The treaty limits the testing and deployment of new defense systems. Russian President Vladimir Putin contends that violating the 1972 treaty will upset nuclear stability and result in a new arms race.

Given these problems and how much it will cost, is NMD a good idea? What is your position?

6. Mini-Nukes

(For more details, see Fred Kaplan, "Low-Yield Nukes," posted November 21, 2003, on http://www.slate.msn.com.)

In 1970, the United States signed the Non-Proliferation Treaty. This Treaty involved a pact between nations having nuclear weapons and nations not having them. Nations not having them promised to not develop nuclear weapons, and nations already having them promised to pursue nuclear disarmament. In 1992 the United States unilaterally stopped nuclear testing, on orders of the first President Bush, and then formalized this in 1995 by signing the Comprehensive Test Ban

Treaty. It prohibits the testing and development of nuclear weapons indefinitely, and it was signed by 186 other nations.

In 2003, the second Bush administration insisted that Iran and North Korea halt their nuclear-weapons programs, and argued that the invasion and occupation of Iraq was justified because Iraq had weapons of mass destruction or WMD, that is, chemical, biological, and nuclear weapons (or at least a nuclear weapons program). Yet at the same time, the second Bush administration was actively developing a new generation of exotic nuclear weapons including low-yield mini nukes and earth-penetrating nukes, despite the fact that the country already had 7,650 nuclear warheads and bombs. Specifically, the Fiscal Year 2004 defense bill, passed by both houses of Congress in November 2003 did four things. First, it repealed the 1992 law banning the development of low-yield nuclear weapons. Second, the bill provided $15 million to develop an earth-penetrating nuclear weapon, a bunker buster. Third, it allocated $6 million to explore special-effects bombs, for example, the neutron bomb that enhances radiation. Finally, the bill provided $25 million for underground nuclear tests.

This renewed development of nuclear weapons and testing violated the 1970 and 1995 Treaties, but the second Bush administration argued that it was necessary to do this for self-defense. The old warheads mounted on intercontinental missiles were designed to wipe out industrial complexes or destroy whole cities. But such weapons were never used, and it appeared that they had no utility. Certainly they were not effective against suicide bombers or other terrorist attacks. What was needed, it was argued, was smaller warheads that could destroy underground bunkers or WMD storage sites.

Critics argued that the U.S. development of more nuclear weapons undermined the attempt to stop similar development in other nations. If the United States needed nuclear weapons for self-defense, then why didn't other nations need them too? The fact that the United States did not attack North Korea (which had nuclear weapons) seemed to support the view that nations needed these weapons to deter attacks.

Furthermore, critics argued that mini-nukes or bunker busters were not necessary. Conventional weapons could do the job. The United States already had at least two non-nuclear smart bombs that could penetrate the earth before exploding. There was the GBU-24, a 2000-pound laser-guided bomb, and the BLU-109 JDAM, a 2000-pound satellite-guided bomb. Both of these bombs could be filled with incendiary explosive that will burn whatever biological or chemical agents might be stored in an underground site.

So why did the United States need to develop more nuclear weapons? Was this necessary or effective for self-defense? Explain your answer. And why did the United States continue to have 7,650 nuclear warheads and bombs? Was it ever necessary to have so many weapons? Is it necessary now? What is your view?

7. The Gulf War

(For a book-length treatment of the Gulf War, including the view of it as jihad, see Kenneth L. Vaux, *Ethics and the Gulf War* [Boulder, CO: Westview Press, 1992].) In August 1990, the Iraqi army invaded and occupied Kuwait. Although the

United States had received warnings, officials did not take them seriously. Saddam Hussein believed the United States would not intervene and apparently had received assurances to that effect. Hussein claimed that the invasion was justified because Kuwait had once been part of Iraq and because the Kuwaitis were exploiting the Rumalla oilfield, which extended into Iraq. The immediate response of the United States and its allies was to begin a ship embargo against Iraq. President George Bush, citing atrocities against the Kuwaitis, compared Hussein to Hitler. For his part, Hussein declared the war to be jihad and threatened the mother of all battles (as he put it) if the Americans dared to intervene. Iran's Ayatollah Khomeini, certainly no friend of the United States, seconded the claim of jihad, adding that anyone killed in battle would be a martyr and immediately go to paradise, the Islamic heaven.

In the months that followed, Iraq ignored repeated ultimatums to leave Kuwait. But Iraq did try to stall for time, following the Koranic teaching of "withholding your hand a little while from war" (Vaux, 1992: 71). Thousands of foreign prisoners were released, and Iraq responded positively to French and Soviet peace initiatives. At the same time, Saddam Hussein continued to call it a holy war, saying that the United States was a satanic force attacking the religious values and practices of Islam.

On January 16, 1991, after a U.N. deadline had passed, the allied forces (American, British, French, Saudi, and Kuwaiti) launched a massive day-and-night air attack on military targets in Iraq, including the capital city of Baghdad. The forty days of air war that followed was very one sided. The allied forces were able to bomb targets at will using advanced technical weapons such as radar-seeking missiles, laser-guided bombs, stealth fighters that avoided radar detection, and smart cruise missiles that could adjust their course. The Iraqi air force never got off the ground, but hid or flew to Iran. The Iraqi Scud missiles killed twenty-two American soldiers sleeping in Saudi Arabia and civilians in Israel but were mostly unreliable and ineffective. Finally, the ground war (Operation Desert Storm) lasted only 100 hours before the allied forces liberated Kuwait City. The Iraqis had more that 200,000 casualties (according to American estimates) while the allied forces sustained less than 200 casualties.

Can this war be justified using the just war theory? Carefully explain your answer. Keep in mind that some religious leaders at the time said that it was not a just war.

Was this really a jihad, as Saddam Hussein and the Ayatollah Khomeini said? Remember that Kuwait and Saudi Arabia are also Muslim countries.

Oil presented another consideration. Kuwait had about 20 percent of the world's known oil reserves at the time. Some said the war was really about the control and price of oil and argued that if Kuwait had not had valuable resources, the United States would not have intervened. (For example, the United States did nothing when China invaded and occupied a defenseless Tibet in 1949.)

8. *Gandhi*

Gandhi's life is beautifully portrayed in the movie Gandhi (1982), directed by Richard Attenborough, with Ben Kingsley as Gandhi. Gandhi's views on war are collected in Madadev Desai, ed., *Nonviolence in Peace and War,* 2 vols. (Ahmedalbad: Navajivan Press, 1945).

Mohandas Gandhi (1869–1948) was the most famous and effective pacifist of the twentieth century. After achieving reforms in the treatment of Hindus and Muslims in South Africa, he returned to India, where he campaigned against British rule, resulting in the departure of the British in 1948, the same year that Gandhi was killed by an orthodox Hindu.

Gandhi was a Hindu who practiced *ahimsa* (nonviolence) toward all living things. (He was considered unorthodox, however, because he rejected the caste system and did not accept everything in the Vedas, the Hindu sacred scriptures.) The concept of ahimsa originated in Jainism and was accepted by both Buddhism and Hinduism. In those religions, ahimsa is understood as not harming any living thing by actions of body, mind, or speech. In Jainism, ahimsa is practiced even with respect to plants, whereas in Hinduism and Buddhism, plants are not included, but nonhuman animals are.

The most original aspect of Gandhi's teaching and methods was what he called *satyagraha* (literally, "truth force"). Satyagraha involves ahimsa and austerities such as fasting. It is supposed to purify one's soul and transform the souls of those it is used against. In practice, the methods of satyagraha developed by Gandhi included marches, demonstrations, sit-ins, strikes, boycotts, fasts, and prayers. These nonviolent and passive methods worked well against the British and have been widely admired and copied. In the United States, Dr. Martin Luther King, Jr. (1929–1968), used similar tactics in the civil rights struggles of the 1950s and 1960s.

Gandhi's nonviolent tactics worked against the British, but would they have been effective against someone like Hitler, who was willing to kill millions of innocent people? Would they stop terrorist attacks such as the September 11 attacks? Is nonviolent resistance an acceptable alternative to war? Is it effective in fighting terrorism? Explain your answers.

Suggested Readings

1. For the official Bush administration view of the War on Terrorism and the Iraq war see the CIA website (http://www.cia.org) and the FBI website (http://www.fbi.org). Both websites are full of information and statements by officials. For pacifist views see http://www.antiwar.com and http://www.nonviolence.org. For an Arab perspective see The Institute for War and Peace Reporting website (http://www.iwpr.net).
2. Hans Blix, *Disarming Iraq* (New York: Pantheon Books, 2004). Blix was the leader of the UN weapons inspection team in Iraq. He concludes that every claim made by the Bush administration about Iraq's weapons program—the mobile biological labs, the yellowcake, the aluminum tubes—has proven to be false, and that the invasion was unnecessary.
3. Christopher Hitchens, *A Long Short War: The Postponed Liberation of Iraq* (London: Plume, 2003), argues that the U.S. invasion of Iraq liberated the Iraqis from oppression, and prevented Iraq from attacking the U.S. with nuclear weapons.
4. Richard A. Clarke, *Against All Enemies* (New York: The Free Press, 2004). Clarke was the counterterrorism coordinator in both the Clinton and second Bush administrations.

He claims that President George W. Bush was obsessed with Iraq after the 9/11 attacks, and eager to blame Iraq even though there was overwhelming evidence that al Qaeda was responsible.

5. Steve Coll, *Ghost Wars* (London: The Penguin Press, 2004), explains the history of al Qaeda in Afghanistan, including how Saudi Arabia aided the rise of Osama bin Laden and Islamic extremism.

6. Ahmed Rashid, *Taliban: Militant Islam, Oil, and Fundamentalism in Central Asia* (New Haven: Yale University Press, 2000), presents the history of the Taliban and explains their version of Islam. They believe they are God's invincible soldiers fighting an unending war against unbelievers.

7. Anthony H. Cordesman, *Terrorism, Asymmetric Warfare, and Weapons of Mass Destruction* (Westport, CT: Praeger, 2001), discusses previous commissions on terrorism, the details of homeland defense, and the risk of chemical and biological attacks.

8. Yossef Bodansky, *Bin Laden: The Man Who Declared War on America* (New York: Random House, 2001). This book is by a well-known expert on terrorism; it covers bin Laden's life and his pursuit of chemical, biological, and nuclear weapons.

9. Paul R. Pillar, *Terrorism and U.S. Foreign Policy* (Washington, DC: Brookings Institution, 2001), explains the causes of modern terrorism in countries such as Pakistan and Afghanistan and examines the new war against terrorism.

10. Peter Partner, *God of Battles: Holy Wars of Christianity and Islam* (Princeton, NJ: Princeton University Press, 1998), explains the doctrines of war in Christianity and Islam.

11. James Turner Johnson, *Mortality and Contemporary Warfare* (New Haven: Yale University Press, 1999), presents the history and development of just war theory and its application in the real world.

12. Bryan Brophy-Baermann and John A. C. Conybeare, "Retaliating against Terrorism," *American Journal of Political Science* 38, 1 (February 1994): 196–210, argue that retaliation against terrorism produces a temporary deviation in attacks but no long-term effect.

13. Dilip Hiro, *Holy Wars: The Rise of Islamic Fundamentalism* (London: Routledge, 1989), explains the development of Islamic fundamentalism found today in Iran and Afghanistan, where Islam has emerged as a radical ideology of armed warfare.

14. Ayatollah Ruhollah Khomeini, "Islam Is Not a Religion of Pacifists," in Amir Taheri, ed., *Holy Terror* (Bethesda, MD: Adler & Adler, 1987), gives a clear statement of the Islamic doctrine of holy war. According to the Ayatollah Khomeini, Islam says, "Kill all the unbelievers just as they would kill you all!"

15. R. Peters, "Jihad," in *The Encyclopedia of Religion* (New York: Macmillan, 1989), gives a scholarly account of the Islamic concept of jihad and its application to war.

16. A. Maalory, *The Crusaders through Arab Eyes* (New York: Schocken Books, 1985), covers two centuries of hostility and war between Muslim Arabs and Christian Crusaders from the West (called Franks), starting with the fall of Jerusalem in 1099. It is a depressing history of invasion, counterinvasion, massacres, and plunder.

17. Michael Walzer, *Just and Unjust Wars: A Moral Argument with Historical Illustrations* (New York: Basic Books, 1977), develops and defends just war theory and applies the theory to numerous historical cases, such as the Six-Day War, the Vietnam War, the Korean War, and World War II. He argues that the Vietnam War can be justified as assistance to the legitimate government of South Vietnam.

18. Robert L. Phillips, *War and Justice* (Norman, OK: University of Oklahoma Press, 1984), defends just war theory. He accepts two principles of the theory, the principle of proportionality and the principle of discrimination. The latter principle, however, in turn rests on the doctrine of double effect, which distinguishes between intending to kill and merely foreseeing that death will occur as an unintended consequence of an action.

19. James Johnson, *The Just War Tradition and the Restraint of War* (Princeton, NJ: Princeton University Press, 1981), explains the historical development of just war theory from the Middle Ages to the present.

20. Paul Ramsey, *The Just War: Force and Political Responsibility* (New York: Charles Scribner's Sons, 1968). This book is a collection of articles on just war theory, all written by Ramsey. He is a Christian who defends a version of the theory that has an absolute principle of discrimination against killing noncombatants. Yet having accepted this principle, he goes on to claim that the war in Vietnam was justified though it involved killing many noncombatants.

21. Paul Christopher, *The Ethics of War and Peace* (Englewood Cliffs, NJ: Prentice-Hall, 1994). This textbook covers the just war tradition, the international laws on war, and moral issues such as war crimes; reprisals; and nuclear, biological, and chemical weapons.

22. Immanuel Kant, *Perpetual Peace* (New York: Liberal Arts Press, 1957). In a classic discussion, Kant maintains that war must not be conducted in a way that rules out future peace. Perpetual peace results when democratic countries let the people decide about going to war. Kant believes that the people will always vote for peace.

23. Albert Schweitzer, *The Teaching of Reverence for Life*, trans. Richard and Clara Masters (New York: Holt, Rinehart and Winston, 1965), argues that all taking of life is wrong because all life is sacred.

24. Leo Tolstoy, *The Law of Love and the Law of Violence*, trans. Mary Koutouzow Tolstoy (New York: Holt, Rinehart and Winston, 1971), explains his Christian pacifism.

25. Mohandas K. Gandhi, "The Practice of Satyagraha," in Ronald Duncan, ed., *Gandhi: Selected Writings* (New York: Harper & Row, 1971), presents his view of nonviolent resistance as an alternative to war.

26. T. R. Miles, "On the Limits to the Use of Force," *Religious Studies* 20 (1984): 113–20, defends a version of pacifism that is opposed to all war but not to all use of force. This kind of pacifism would require one to refuse to serve in the military but would not rule out serving as a police officer.

27. William Earle, "In Defense of War," *The Monist* 57, 4 (October 1973): 561–69 attacks pacifism (defined as the principled opposition to all war) and then gives a justification for the morality and rationality of war.

28. Jan Narveson, "In Defense of Peace," in Jan Narveson, ed., *Moral Issues* (Oxford: Oxford University Press, 1983), pp. 59–71, replies to Earle. He does not defend pacifism; instead, he argues that whenever there is a war, at least one party is morally unjustified.

29. Jan Narveson, "Morality and Violence: War, Revolution, Terrorism," in Tom Regan, ed., *Matters of Life and Death: New Introductory Essays in Moral Philosophy* (New York: McGraw Hill, 1993), pp. 121–159. In this survey article, Narveson covers many different issues, including the nature and morality of violence, the right of self-defense, pacifism, just war theory, and terrorism.

30. Richard A. Wasserstrom, ed., *War and Morality* (Belmont, CA: Wadsworth, 1970), is a collection of articles on the morality of war and other issues. Elizabeth Anscombe discusses the doctrine of double effect as it applies to war. Wasserstrom argues that modern wars are very difficult to justify because innocents are inevitably killed.

31. Jean Bethke Elshtain, *Women and War* (New York: Basic Books, 1987). What is the feminist view of war? According to Elshtain, some feminists are pacifists working for world peace, whereas others want to reject the traditional noncombatant role of women and become warriors. As a result of the second position, the United States now has a higher percentage of women in the military than any other industrialized nation.

Index